BRITISH COLUMBIA HISTORY

Intriguing and Entertaining Facts
about our Province's Past

Mark Thorburn

BLUE
BIKE
BOOKS

The Publisher: Blue Bike Books

Library and Archives Canada Cataloguing in Publication

Thorburn, Mark
   Bathroom book of British Columbia history : intriguing and enter-
taining facts about our province's past / Mark Thorburn ; Roger Garcia,
Pat Bidwell, illustrators.

(Bathroom books of Canada ; 7)
ISBN-13: 978-1-897278-15-4
ISBN-10: 1-897278-15-2

1. British Columbia—History—Miscellanea. I. Garcia, Roger,
1976– II. Title. III. Series.
FC3811.T56 2006   971.1   C2006-904129-6

Project Director: Nicholle Carrière
Project Editor: Nicholle Carrière
Illustrations: Pat Bidwell, Roger Garcia
Cover Image: Pat Bidwell
PC: P5

We acknowledge the support of the Alberta Foundation for the Arts for
our publishing program.

 Canadian Heritage Patrimoine canadien

DEDICATION
To my parents, Bev and Gary

ACKNOWLEDGEMENTS

Thank you to Blue Bike Books for the opportunity to work on this project; to my editor, Nicholle Carrière, for her wonderful skill and tremendous insights; to my heroes, Pierre Berton, Bruce Catton and David McCullough, and to my friends and professors, Bernard Burke, Jim Heath and Peter Moogk, for teaching me that history does not have to be boring and dull, but can be exciting and fun; and to my girlfriend, Debbie, for her never-ending encouragement, support, patience and understanding and without whom this project would never have succeeded.

CONTENTS

IN THE BEGINNING...

GOLD RUSHES AND MINING

POST-CONFEDERATION EVENTS

LITERATURE, MUSIC AND MOVIES

SPORTS

PROGRESS COMES TO BRITISH COLUMBIA

BUSINESS, FINANCE AND PROHIBITION

OTHER STUFF

THE THREE PM'S

Canada's First Prime Minister...from Victoria!

The first prime minister of Canada to be elected from British Columbia was the Father of Confederation himself, Sir John A. Macdonald. In the 1878 election, Macdonald's Conservative Party defeated the Liberals, but Macdonald was himself beaten in his old riding of Kingston, Ontario, and needed a seat in the House of Commons from somewhere else to keep his job as PM. Fortunately, the voters of Victoria were glad to oblige. British Columbia voted in the federal election that year a month later than the rest of the country. (In the 1870s and 1880s, members of Parliament from Canada's two western provinces, British Columbia and Manitoba, were elected after the rest of the country cast its ballots.)

Hearing of Macdonald's predicament, some residents of Victoria placed Macdonald's name into nomination, and he was elected as their MP. Ironically, since members of Parliament do not have to live in the ridings that they represent, and because the transcontinental railroad was not yet completed, it was not until 1886 that "Old Tomorrow" ever set foot in British Columbia and saw Victoria for the first time.

Mrs. Macdonald Sees BC from the Top of a Cowcatcher!

In 1886, a year after BC was linked to the rest of Canada by the transcontinental railway, Sir John A. Macdonald became the first prime minister to visit British Columbia. Macdonald was accompanied by his young, adventurous wife, Agnes. They travelled west by train to Port Moody and then sailed to Victoria. (The train tracks did not yet go as far as Vancouver.) And for the last 1000 kilometres of the trip, from Laggan Station (near Lake Louise) to Port Moody, Mrs. Macdonald chose an unusual place to ride: on the cowcatcher of the train!

Tired of viewing the scenery from inside, Agnes sat from dawn to dusk and again for hours in the dark after dinner on an empty candle box that was placed in front of the engine on the buffer beam. Her husband thought the idea was "rather ridiculous," and with the train tracks skirting the edges of 45-metre-high cliffs, entering dark tunnels and going across creaky bridges, it was a dangerous way to travel. Agnes was often alone on the cowcatcher with only a soft felt hat on her head, a linen carriage-cover covering her from waist to foot, and an umbrella and a "waterproof" in hand whenever the train went through a tunnel. At the end of the day, Mrs. Macdonald's face and dress were normally covered with ash from the train's smokestack. Despite all this, Agnes thought that the experience was "lovely" and only when there was a possibility of a landslide was she persuaded to ride inside.

Flying Pig Almost Kills
PM's Aide!

Agnes Macdonald's famous 1886 ride on the cowcatcher of the train from Lake Louise to Port Moody was a dangerous way to travel. Sir John A. Macdonald's wife normally rode alone at the front of the train, but the prime minister, the superintendent of the railroad and some of the younger members of the PM's staff sometimes shared the adventure with her. Once, while Mrs. Macdonald and the prime minister's assistant, Joseph Pope, were riding on the cowcatcher, Pope was almost killed when the train hit a pig, and the animal's body flew between him and the post he was holding onto.

Grandson of Rossland Sits as Prime Minister

The second prime minister of Canada who hailed from British Columbia (well, sort of) was John Turner. His mother was a native of Rossland and the chancellor of the University of British Columbia, and his stepfather was the lieutenant-governor of the province. Also, though he was born in England, Turner spent his teenage years in British Columbia and was a graduate of the University of British Columbia. However, after law school, he pursued a successful legal and political career in Ontario and Québec. When Pierre Trudeau retired in 1984, Turner was chosen to be the new Liberal Party leader and became prime minister. However, he did not at that time have a seat in the House of Commons. In the election that year, Turner was elected to Parliament from Vancouver Quadra, but the Liberals suffered a massive defeat and Conservative Brian Mulroney became prime minister. So, when Turner assumed his British Columbia seat in the House of Commons, it was as an ex-prime minister who was now the leader of the Opposition.

What Province is He From?

John Turner is one of only two people in Canadian history to represent three provinces in the House of Commons. (The other person to accomplish this feat was Prime Minister William Lyon Mackenzie King.) Besides British Columbia, Turner also represented Ontario and Québec in Parliament at various times in his career.

More Than Just a Mom

British Columbian Phyllis Gregory was much more than just the mother of Prime Minister John Turner. The daughter of a Rossland miner, she was one of the first female graduates of the University of British Columbia and later studied economics in the United States, Germany and Great Britain. Gregory worked as an economist for the federal government during the Great Depression and became the most senior woman in Canada's civil service. Widowed at a young age, one of her suitors before she remarried was Prime Minister R.B. Bennett. Gregory eventually wed multimillionaire and future lieutenant-governor of British Columbia, Frank Ross. Awarded both the Order of the British Empire and the Order of Canada, she became the chancellor of UBC and the first woman chancellor of a university in the Commonwealth in 1961. Unfortunately, Gregory suffered from Alzheimer's disease later in life and never knew that her son was prime minister.

Port Alberni Girl Makes Good!

If you count both John A. Macdonald and John Turner, the third prime minister from British Columbia (and the first one actually born in the province) was Kim Campbell. Born in Port Alberni, raised in Burnaby and Vancouver and educated at the University of British Columbia, her rise in politics was meteoric. Campbell was elected to the Vancouver School Board (while she was still in law school) in 1980, to the British Columbia Legislative Assembly in 1986 and to the House of Commons in 1988. Once in Parliament, she was appointed by Prime Minister Brian Mulroney to serve as minister of state for Indian affairs and northern development in 1989, minister of justice in 1990 and minister of national defence in 1993. Campbell succeeded Mulroney as prime minister in June 1993, but her residency at 24 Sussex Drive was short-lived; she and her Conservative Party were defeated in a landslide by Jean Chrètien and the Liberals the following October.

DID YOU  KNOW?

Kim Campbell has been divorced more times (twice) than any other prime minister of Canada. In 1972, she married University of British Columbia mathematics professor, author, local politician and international chess champion Nathan Divinsky (who was 21 years Campbell's senior). They were divorced in 1983. In 1986, Campbell married a man much closer to her own age, American-born Vietnam veteran, former UBC law professor and provincial and federal government attorney, Howard Eddy. That marriage ended in 1993, before Campbell became prime minister. Since 1997, Campbell has lived in the United States with Canadian-born actor and composer Hershey Felder (who is 21 years Campbell's junior), and they are registered as common-law spouses with the Department of Foreign Affairs.

FAMILY TIES

Pierre Trudeau

Although he was from Québec, Prime Minister Pierre Trudeau had a number of family connections to British Columbia. His wife, Margaret, was born in Vancouver. His father-in-law, James Sinclair, was a prominent civil engineer who represented BC in the House of Commons from 1940 to 1958 and served in Prime Minister Louis St. Laurent's cabinet. And, tragically, Trudeau's youngest son, Michel, was killed in an avalanche near Kokanee Lake.

Charles Tupper

Prime Minister Charles Tupper's descendants may have been Nova Scotians from way back, but one branch of the Tupper family has strong ties to Vancouver. The prime minister's son, Charles Hibbert Tupper, was a Nova Scotia politician, federal cabinet minister and attorney who moved to Vancouver in 1897. While continuing to represent Pictou, Nova Scotia, in the House of Commons, Charles established a prominent law firm in Vancouver that continues to this very day. He later turned down the lieutenant-governorship of British Columbia. Prime Minister Tupper's grandson, Reginald Hibbert Tupper, was a World War I hero and noted Vancouver lawyer whom the BC government appointed to investigate charges of corruption in the Vancouver Police Department. And Tupper's great-grandson, Charles Cecil Ingersoll Merritt, another famous Vancouver attorney, won the Victoria Cross for heroism at Dieppe in World War II (Canada's first in the war). He spent three years in Germany as a prisoner of war and later represented British Columbia in the House of Commons.

Mackenzie Bowell

While Prime Minister Mackenzie Bowell was still the federal minister of customs, his son, John Moore Bowell, was appointed in 1887 to serve as Vancouver's first Collector of Customs. It was probably the most important federal job in Vancouver at the time, and John held the post for 30 years. The prime minister's grandson and namesake, Mackenzie Bowell, became a multimillionaire while working for 50 years as a Vancouver automobile retail salesman; he owned what eventually became the largest Buick, Cadillac and Pontiac dealership in Canada. The younger Mackenzie Bowell also opened Canada's first used car supermarket in 1954 and was, for two years, the president of the Pacific National Exhibition (the famous "PNE").

John Abbott

Prime Minister John Abbott's brother, Harry Braithwaite Abbott, was a famous railroad engineer who played a prominent role in the construction of the transcontinental railway that connected BC with the rest of Canada. Later moving to Vancouver in 1886, Harry was also in charge of the Canadian Pacific Railway's General Pacific Division, was the president of the Vancouver and Lulu Island Railroad (which linked Vancouver to Steveston) and was the owner of a large ranch in the Nicola Valley. Although it is a misspelling of his name, the city of Abbotsford is named after him. And Harry's sons both made their mark in British Columbia. The eldest, John Louis Grahame Abbott, was a prominent Rossland and Vancouver attorney while the youngest, Harry Hamilton Abbott, was a long-time BC rancher.

JUST THE FACTS

A Man's Job?

Thirty-two men, but only one woman, have been premier of British Columbia since the province joined Confederation in 1871.

I Thought He'd Never Leave!

The shortest-serving premier was Joseph Martin, who held the office for only three months and 14 days (106 days) in 1900.

The longest-serving premier was William Andrew Cecil "W.A.C." Bennett, who served for 20 years, one month and 14 days (7351 days) from 1952 to 1972.

It's Getting Crowded Here!

Of British Columbia's 24 dead former premiers, 12 of them are buried at Victoria's Ross Bay Cemetery.

Youth Has Its Advantages

The youngest premier in British Columbia history was Richard McBride, who was only 32 years, 6 months and 16 days old when he assumed office in 1903. He was also the first native-born British Columbian to hold the job, remarkably handsome and popular, and so far, the only BC premier to be knighted.

Golden Oldies

The oldest person to become premier of British Columbia was John Robson, who was 65 years, 4 months and 19 days old when he assumed office in 1889. The oldest departing premier was W.A.C. Bennett, who left office nine days after his 72nd birthday in 1972.

They Weren't All Native Sons

Of BC's 33 premiers, only eight were born in the province. Eleven were born elsewhere in Canada, seven in England and four in Ireland. The remaining three were born in the United States (James Dunsmuir), the Netherlands (Bill Vander Zalm) and India (Ujjal Dosanjh).

Big Simon
The largest premier of BC was Simon Tolmie, who weighed in at 136 kilograms!

Short Bill

The shortest premier of BC was William Bowser. who was only 157 centimetres tall!

No Party Politics in British Columbia?
Before 1903, there were no formal party politics in British Columbia, and most candidates for the Legislative Assembly were elected as individuals rather than as the nominees of any party. That meant there was little or no discipline in the legislature, a premier's ability to govern depended on constantly shifting personal and political allegiances, and a government could fall at any time over any issue. As a result, between 1871 and 1903, there was a new premier, on average, every two years!

Honest Andrew

When Andrew Charles Elliott became premier in 1876, he already had a well-established reputation for honesty. When his appointment by the lieutenant-governor was announced, the *Daily British Colonist* and *Victoria Chronicle* exclaimed: "Nearly 20 years in office and not rich!"

Survived Terrible Nazi Occupation

Premier Bill Vander Zalm knew better than most about the terrible atrocities of the Nazis. Born in Noordwykerhout, the Netherlands, he grew up in Nazi-occupied Holland during World War II.

Madam Premier

The first (and, so far, only) female premier of British Columbia was Rita Johnston, who succeeded Bill Vander Zalm on April 2, 1991. She was also the first woman premier in Canada. Originally elected to the provincial legislature in 1983, she held various posts in Vander Zalm's cabinet before becoming the political leader of the province. Her tenure as BC's highest public official, however, was short-lived; only six months after taking office, she and her Social Credit government were defeated at the polls.

Family Ties

W.A.C. Bennett, who was BC's premier from 1952 to 1972, and William Richards Bennett, who was premier from 1975 to 1986, were father and son.

Alexander Edmund Batson "A.E.B." Davie, who was BC's premier from 1887 to 1889, and Theodore Davie, who was premier from 1892 to 1895, were brothers.

At Least They Weren't Murdered!

To date, five premiers have died in office. Surprisingly, in light of how heated BC politics can get, no premier has been assassinated.

Crushed Pinkie Causes Death

News flash: June 29, 1892. Premier John Robson dies in London, England! The cause of death: blood poisoning that set in after the tip of his little finger was crushed when the door of a hansom taxicab (a type of horse-drawn carriage) slammed on it. Robson was the third premier in a row to die in office.

Previously, William Smithe had died in 1887 (of nephritis, a kidney disease) and A.E.B. Davie in 1889 (of phthisis, a consumptive disease). The only other premiers to die in office were Harlan Brewster (of pneumonia in 1918) and John Oliver (of cancer in 1927).

It's a Matter of Faith

Most of BC's premiers have been Christian. Dave Barrett (1972–75) was the province's first Jewish premier and Ujjal Dosanjh (2000–01) its first Sikh premier.

Dewdney Dick

While he was leader of the Opposition, the press often referred to Richard McBride as "Dewdney Dick" because he represented the riding of Westminster-Dewdney in the Legislative Assembly. When McBride became premier in 1903, at 32 years of age, he was young, good-looking and highly personable, with long, flowing, white hair and an amazing ability to charm voters. He also had the good luck to preside over a booming economy that made him the most popular man in the province. As premier, McBride acquired some new nicknames, including "Handsome Dick," "the People's Dick" and "Glad-hand Dick."

It's Miller Time!

When Dan Miller became premier after Glen Clark's sudden departure in 1999, he did not want the job and accepted it only with the understanding that the appointment would be temporary until the New Democratic Party elected a permanent party leader. Miller was known to occasionally enjoy a beer or two and that led pundits to refer to his six months in office as "Miller Time in BC"!

Building Bridges

Premier Duff Pattullo used a welding torch in 1937 to cut a chain-link barrier at the ceremony opening the New Westminster Bridge that bears his name. Since there was originally a toll to be paid for driving over the bridge, critics and local residents often called it the "Pay-Toll-O" Bridge.

AMOR DE COSMOS

So What Does a Name Matter?

Ever hear of William Alexander Smith? No? Well, how about Amor De Cosmos? Smith wanted a name that reflected what he loved the most: "order, beauty, the world and the universe." So the future premier of British Columbia had his name legally changed to Amor De Cosmos when he lived in California in 1854. (Smith had arrived in the Golden State the year before to join in the California Gold Rush.) The new moniker was frequently the butt of jokes and jeers, but it was definitely more memorable than plain, old Bill Smith.

What Shall We Call Him?

California's lawmakers had a field day while they were considering legislation to change William Alexander Smith's name to Amor De Cosmos. (Statutes, rather than court decrees, were the way to legally change one's name back then.) Poking fun at Smith's desire for a new identity, the legislators proposed amendments to the bill that would have named the future BC premier "Amor Muggins Cosmos" and "Amor De Cosmos Caesar." But the amendments failed; Smith's original proposal was silly enough.

DID YOU KNOW?

Although the California statute that legally changed William Smith's name to Amor De Cosmos used a small "d," De Cosmos signed his name with a capital one. Also, until 1870, he followed the "D" with the Greek letter epsilon (ε) rather than with a small "e."

Make Sure You Get My Name Right!

The political opponents of Amor De Cosmos (the former Bill Smith) once successfully argued to election officials that his name change was legal only in California. As a result, when De Cosmos ran for election to the Vancouver Island colonial legislature in 1860, he was forced to run as "William Alexander Smith commonly known as Amor De Cosmos." There was no secret ballot back in those days; instead, voters had to publicly announce who they were voting for, and they had to get their candidate's name right or their vote did not count. De Cosmos lost that election by a single vote when one person simply but incorrectly answered "Amor De Cosmos" when asked who his ballot was cast for.

Our Man in Victoria

Amor De Cosmos was premier of British Columbia for 13 and a half months (December 23, 1872 to February 9, 1874). Most of that time, he was not in Victoria, or even in BC, but in Ottawa (he was also a member of Parliament) or London, England (where he was dealing with the Brits on provincial matters). So who was in charge when De Cosmos was away? Attorney General George Walkem.

BC's Own Father of Confederation

Although the idea was still unpopular in British Columbia, Amor De Cosmos strongly supported the colony's union with the new Dominion of Canada. Indeed, because of his role behind BC's entry into Canada in 1871, he is often called "British Columbia's Father of Confederation." But De Cosmos slowly came to believe that the federal government was not living up to its end of the deal that led to BC's joining the new nation. In 1879, as a member of Parliament, De Cosmos introduced a motion in the House of Commons to separate British Columbia from Canada.

The Insane De Cosmos

Premier Amor De Cosmos was one of British Columbia's most eccentric politicians. Emotional and highly opinionated, he would burst into tears while speaking before a crowd. De Cosmos was also known for brawling in public with his fists and walking stick, applying black shoe polish to his beard and refusing to ride tramcars because he was afraid of electricity. George Walkem, who served as attorney general under De Cosmos, described his boss as a man who had "all the eccentricities of a comet but none of the brilliance." Later in life, De Cosmos' actions became even more odd, and his speeches were totally incoherent. Eventually, he was declared insane.

JOSEPH MARTIN

A Very Unique Fellow

Premier Joseph Martin is the only person in Canadian history to serve as a member of two provincial legislatures, as the attorney general of two provinces and as a member of both the Canadian and British Houses of Commons. In 1883, he was elected to the Manitoba legislature and served as attorney general under Premier Thomas Greenway. (It was Martin who drafted the legislation to end French language instruction and government support for Catholic schools in that province, thus starting the Manitoba Schools Crisis that dominated federal politics during the 1890s.) In 1893, he was elected to the House of Commons from Winnipeg. Four years later, Martin moved to British Columbia and was elected to the BC legislature in 1898. He served briefly as attorney general under Premier Charles Semlin, and after living in British Columbia for only three months, became premier himself in 1900. He spent only a short time in office, though—his tenure was a mere three and a half months. In 1908, Martin moved to England and was a member of the British House of Commons from 1910 until 1918. While still in England, he unsuccessfully ran for mayor of Vancouver in 1915.

Nobody Loves Me!

When Lieutenant-Governor Thomas McInnes fired Premier Charles Semlin and replaced him with Joseph Martin in 1900, the BC Legislative Assembly voted 28 to 1 against Martin's appointment. Needless to say, Martin cast the sole dissenting vote. Realizing that he could not garner enough support in the legislature to govern, Martin resigned, an election was called and James Dunsmuir became the next premier.

A Man of Peace

Described by his contemporaries as "volcanic, dramatic, irascible" and as a "hot-blooded fire-eater," Joseph "Fighting Joe" Martin earned his nickname because of his willingness to resort to fisticuffs in public when confronting his opponents. Even public religious events were not exempt from his propensity to start a fight. In 1902, during prayers at the provincial legislature, the former premier got into a fistfight with Richard McBride over which of them would become Opposition leader.

WILLIAM BOWSER

A Very "Short" Man

Standing only about 157 centimetres tall, William Bowser was British Columbia's shortest premier. He was also short on political ethics. While attorney general and minister of finance in Premier Richard McBride's cabinet, Bowser brought BC politics to one of its lowest points. He created and financed a powerful political machine through the liberal use of patronage and bribery, and he was not above using the occasional threat.

Bowser controlled the city police and politicians in Vancouver and Victoria and threw around money to influence public officials elsewhere in the province. As a cabinet minister, Bowser made sure that plenty of work was sent to his law firm by the government. He even caused saloons to lose their liquor licences if they could not persuade their patrons to vote Conservative. And Bowser's tactics introduced a new word to the dictionary: "Bowserism."

Not A Very Loveable Fellow

Premier William Bowser was a cold, ruthless and corrupt politician with an ill temper, dour exterior and abrupt manner. Fortunately, his tenure as premier (1915–16) was short-lived, but he was for many years the provincial attorney general and minister of finance under his predecessor and old college chum, Premier Richard McBride, and he was considered by many to be the man behind McBride's throne. Bowser was certainly the person to see whenever the premier was out of town, which McBride frequently was. Even many fellow Conservatives could not stomach Bowser and his methods. Charles Hibbert Tupper, a prominent Vancouver lawyer and son of a prime minister, called him "Little Kaiser," which was not a compliment in light of the poor relations at the time between Germany and the British Empire. (The two countries went to war in 1914.) Bowser was also called the "Napoleon of British Columbia" and a few other names that are not printable here. The only reason that Bowser became premier was because McBride suddenly resigned amid charges of corruption before an election was called and there was no one else to take charge.

JOHN OLIVER

Honest John

John Oliver, BC's premier from 1918 to 1927, was known as "Honest John" because of his strong sense of personal integrity. A farmer from Delta, he often wore overalls at work, kept an old, battered alarm clock on his office wall and drank tea out of a saucer whenever he felt like it. Oliver was also well known for his thriftiness. Once, while visiting Vancouver, he wouldn't stay at the luxurious Hotel Vancouver, but slept at much cheaper accommodations down the road. And while riding a train on official business to Ottawa, the premier booked a lower berth rather than avail himself of a more expensive private compartment or drawing room like his ministers did.

Generous Benefactor

Premier John Oliver was famous for his acts of kindness. One day, as he was leaving the parliament buildings in Victoria, Oliver came across a poorly dressed lad who was selling newspapers to the politicians and civil servants as they headed home from work. The premier asked the boy a few questions and discovered that a desire for adventure had caused the youngster to leave his job at a Fraser Valley farm and head to Victoria without a cent in his pocket. The young man now regretted his decision. Oliver told the boy to "follow me and jump into this car" and proceeded to drive him to the Oliver residence in Victoria. The premier and his wife put the boy up for the night, and the next day, Oliver took his guest with him to Vancouver. In Vancouver, the pair met Oliver's son, whom the premier had called the night before, and the premier gave the kid a job at the Oliver family farm in Delta.

Merry Christmas!

John Oliver twice played Santa Claus while he was premier. The first time, one cold and wet Christmas Eve, a young man had been arrested on a minor charge and incarcerated in the Victoria jail. Somebody called the premier at his home and told him about the lad. Oliver dropped everything and drove to the police station, where he had the boy released by promising to personally bring the youngster back for trial. The premier then took the boy to the Oliver home in Victoria, where the young man spent the rest of the night as well as Christmas Day with the premier and his wife. The boy was later tried on the charges and acquitted.

On another Christmas Eve, Oliver learned of an old man living in a shack on a "starve-acre" lot. The poverty-stricken gentleman was not able to earn enough to pay his property taxes, and the delinquency had reached the point that he was about to lose his home (as little as it was). The premier got into his car and drove on rutted roads through heavy forest until he found the shack and its occupant. Once he had confirmed the story, Oliver went back to Victoria and had the taxes struck off the record so the old man could keep his home.

Land Developer

With thousands of soldiers returning to British Columbia after World War I, Premier John Oliver successfully campaigned for the provincial government's purchase of 8900 hectares in the Okanagan Valley to be resold, at favourable terms, to any veteran who wished to settle there. Oliver also obtained the construction of a gravity-fed irrigation ditch to bring water to the then-semiarid region. In appreciation for what the premier had done, the residents of the new community named their town "Oliver."

Words of Wisdom from Premier John Oliver

☛ "The hog that gets fat first is usually killed first."

☛ "Sometimes it requires more courage to stand still than go forward."

☛ "The man on top of the stack has the widest view, but he gets all the wind and flying ants."

☛ "No man is a whit bigger than his soul, whether digging a ditch in overalls or addressing the legislature in a tailored suit."

W.A.C. BENNETT

He's Wacky!

William Andrew Cecil Bennett, BC's longest-serving premier (1952–72), was usually referred to as W.A.C. Bennett. Personally, he went by the name Cecil or "Cece." But he was also known, by friend and foe alike, as "Wacky" Bennett. (And so were many of his ideas!)

British Columbia Plus the Yukon?

One of Premier "Wacky" Bennett's ideas was to replace Canada's 10 provinces with five: the Atlantic, Québec, Ontario, the Prairies (which would include most of the Northwest Territories and present-day Nunavut) and British Columbia (which would include the Yukon). Bennett shocked the country with this proposal at the 1969 constitutional conference in Ottawa, but it went nowhere. However, the suggestion did earn him another nickname: the "Jolly Green Giant."

All Alone

When backbencher W.A.C. Bennett crossed the aisle in the Legislative Assembly in 1951 to become a member of the Social Credit Party, he dramatically increased the Socreds' representation in the legislature—to one!

Make Me Your Leader

Bill Bennett was not elected leader of the provincial Social Credit Party until one month after the 1952 election (which the Socreds won). During the campaign, their temporary leader was Ernest Hansell, who was a member of Parliament—from Alberta!

A True Party Animal

W.A.C. Bennett held one heck of a party at his hometown of Kelowna on August 1, 1959. It was exactly seven years after he had become premier, and by coincidence, BC's government had been officially declared debt-free just the day before. Over 500 guests were invited. Bennett's highways minister, Phil Gaglardi, directed a group of children in singing "Happy Birthday" to the premier, even though Bennett's birthday wasn't for another month. Cabinet members were given toy musical instruments and ordered to play. A swimming race was held between four young contestants, each representing the leader of one of BC's political parties, and Bennett's double easily won with the help of a hidden towrope. And at the end of it all, Bennett and his ministers boarded a launch and sailed out into Lake Okanagan, where a barge waited with $70 million in cancelled government bonds mixed with straw and gasoline and held down by chicken wire. With a bow in hand, Bennett shot a flaming arrow at the bonds. The arrow hit the wire and ricocheted into the water, but a nearby RCMP officer, out of sight of those on shore, ignited the bonds and a giant bonfire ensued during which Bennett played a fiddle just as Nero did when Rome burned.

Since Bennett was both premier and minister of finance and didn't share much information about the government's finances with anyone (including his own cabinet and the legislature), few really knew whether the province was debt-free or not. Indeed, it wasn't until 1965 that the truth came out. While the government's direct debt had been paid off, it was only after $44 million in unpaid bills had been transferred to crown corporations and pub-lic agencies and thus were no longer a direct government liability.

Free Enterprise on the High Seas

For "pro–free enterprise" Premier W.A.C. Bennett, the provincial government would get involved in public projects only when the private sector did not step up to what he thought was needed for BC's well-being and development. For example, in 1958, there were only two ferry lines connecting Vancouver and Victoria, and union disputes closed both of them down. Bennett tried to resolve the problems in order to avert economic disaster but failed. Therefore, without consulting the provincial legislature, he arranged for the government to buy one of the lines for $7.8 million (a price that he dictated and forced on the ferry line). Suddenly, BC was in the ferry business! "Bennett's Navy," as his detractors called it, originally started with only two ships, but within 20 years the British Columbia Ferry Corporation had become the largest ferry service in the world.

The "Castro of BC"

During the 1960 provincial election, Commonwealth Cooperative Federation (CCF) leader Robert Strachen (who wanted to replace W.A.C. Bennett as premier) campaigned on the issue of making the BC Electric Railway Company, Canada's largest privately owned power company and the greatest supplier of electricity in the province, a publicly owned utility. Because of this, the press labelled Strachen the "Fidel Castro of BC." (Cuba's Communist leader at this time was a very scary figure to most North Americans and had just begun to expropriate foreign-owned lands and businesses in his country.) Strachen and the CCF were defeated, but less than a year later, the "pro–free enterprise" government of Premier Bennett adopted Strachen's idea and took over BC Electric for the price of $197 million. The power company later became part of BC Hydro.

Needed Some Legal Experience First

In 1952, Premier W.A.C. Bennett named 32-year-old Robert Bonner as attorney general of British Columbia, though Bonner had graduated from law school only four years earlier! Perhaps Bennett thought it would be a good idea to give his friend some experience before Bonner opened his own law practice. Bonner went on to serve in the post for 16 years before becoming chairman of MacMillan Bloedel and BC Hydro.

Quotes From W.A.C. Bennett:

☛ "The finest sound in the land is the ring of cash registers."

☛ On the New Democratic Party: "They couldn't run a peanut stand."

☛ On the eve of his government's defeat by the New Democratic Party in the 1972 election: "I want to tell you tonight that the socialist hordes are at the gates of British Columbia!"

☛ On why he was politically successful: "I'm plugged into God."

☛ Bennett's response to complaints about the odours emitted by a pulp mill: "It's the smell of money."

Quotes About W.A.C. Bennett:

☛ "One of the most courageous and imaginative political leaders I have ever known."

—Gordon Shrum, co-chair of BC Hydro

☛ "He was the only man I ever knew who could get money from the rich and votes from the poor with the promise to protect them from each other."

—Tommy Douglas, New Democratic Party leader

☛ "During 20 years under Social Credit [i.e., Bennett's administration], this province's physical face was scarred permanently by the actions of a government intent on pursuing economic growth in the cowboy tradition of the frontier."

—*The Vancouver Province*

THE McINNES AFFAIR

Hiring and Firing Premiers

The lieutenant-governor is the monarch's representative in British Columbia and, in theory, the most powerful public official in the province. In reality, the days when the lieutenant-governor exercised any real political power are long gone. But twice Lieutenant-Governor Thomas McInnes fired and hired premiers of British Columbia—John H. Turner for Charles Semlin in 1898 and Semlin for Joseph Martin in 1900—without dissolving the provincial legislature and calling for an election to determine the will of the people. Turner made some noise when he was axed, but nothing came of it. But only hours after his dismissal on February 27, 1900, Semlin declared that McInnes' actions were unconstitutional (they weren't, just unpopular) and introduced in the BC legislature what amounted to a motion of censure of the lieutenant-governor. That resolution was adopted by a vote of 22 to 15. Shortly afterwards, the BC Legislative Assembly formally asked Prime Minister Wilfrid Laurier to dismiss McInnes. That was done on June 20, 1900, making McInnes the only lieutenant-governor in BC history to be fired.

Importing a Lieutenant-Governor

When Prime Minister Laurier dismissed BC Lieutenant-Governor Thomas McInnes, the PM went to Québec to find a replacement. The man he chose was former Québec premier Henri-Gustave Joly de Lotbinière, who had no affiliation with any of British Columbia's political factions. During Joly de Lotbinière's tenure, political stability was returned to the province.

THE "RIGHT" TO VOTE

You Can't Vote!

From 1878 to 1883, schoolteachers were legally prohibited from voting in British Columbia. Other groups who were, at one time or another, ineligible to vote in BC were Canadians of Chinese, Japanese or First Nations descent, as well as "Hindus" (the term was used in a racial sense), Doukhobors, Mennonites, Hutterites, provincial civil servants, judges, magistrates, police, soldiers, sailors, conscientious objectors, anyone working for the federal government (except postal employees) and, of course, women. Also, while they were never prohibited from voting, members of the clergy were once prohibited from running for political office in British Columbia. And to be removed from the voters' list meant more than just being denied the right to vote. It also meant that the person could not run for political office nor, in most cases, become a lawyer, pharmacist or chartered accountant.

Brits Say Asians Can't Vote in BC!

You would think that Tomekichi Homma would have had every right to vote in British Columbia. After all, he was a naturalized citizen and a successful businessman (fisherman and labour contractor). Homma was also fluent in three languages. A community leader, he was one of the organizers of a fisherman's union and one of the founders of the first hospital in Steveston. Homma also started the first Japanese language school in BC and the first Japanese language newspaper in the Vancouver area. But in 1900, the Collector of Voters refused to put Homma's name on the voter's list, so Homma sued the provincial government—and he won! Both the BC and federal courts held that British Columbia's ban against voting by citizens of Asian descent was unconstitutional. But the BC government fought on and appealed to the British Privy Council. (Until 1949, the Privy Council was Canada's final court of appeal.)

And in 1902, the Privy Council overruled the BC and Canadian courts and upheld British Columbia's right to keep Homma from the ballot box. Homma would die 43 years later, shortly after World War II, at Lemon Creek (near Slocan) in an internment camp for Japanese Canadians.

DID YOU KNOW?

Unlike other ethnic groups, blacks were never denied the vote in British Columbia.

But She's a Woman!

The fight for women's suffrage in British Columbia had a lot of false starts. The ladies were first allowed to vote for school trustees in 1884 if they met certain property qualifications. That right was taken away in 1891 but given back a year later. Women won the right to vote in municipal elections in 1906, but the privilege was withdrawn in 1908. The law was changed in 1917 to allow women to vote in both municipal and provincial elections. Later that same year, at the height of the First World War, the right to vote in federal elections was given to women who were in the military or who had relatives in the armed forces. All women except those who were of Asian or First Nations descent or who faced some other disqualification were finally given the right to vote in federal elections in 1918.

DID YOU KNOW?

Until 1985, having Canadian citizenship and being a British Columbia resident wasn't a good enough to be eligible to vote in BC; you had to be a British subject, too. The term "British subject" legally became obsolete in Canada in 1977.

Are You Alive?

In 1900, John Kirkup, former sheriff and the BC government agent and gold commissioner in Rossland, sent the following letter to a dead man in care of the attorney who was settling the deceased's estate:

Dear Sir,

I am to inform you that objection has been taken to your name remaining upon the voters' list for the Rossland Riding of West Kootenay, upon the ground that you have been dead for some time. You will kindly let me know by return mail whether you are dead or not. If you are dead, let me know, and I will strike your name off, but if not, of course your name will remain as is.

ON ELECTION DAY

I Can't Give You a Button,
But I Want Your Vote

Until 1953, it was illegal in British Columbia for a candidate for political office to provide any entertainment, music, buttons, flags, ribbons and cockades within eight days of an election.

Must Be Sober to Vote!

Until 1977, it was illegal to sell liquor in British Columbia on Election Day.

Who Are You Voting For?
From 1940 to 1982, public opinion polls gauging the popularity of political parties and their candidates during a provincial election were illegal in British Columbia.

And the Winner Is...

In the 1875 provincial election, there was a three-way tie in the election for MLA from the Kootenay riding (something that has never happened before or since in BC). To break the tie, the riding's recording officer cast the deciding vote.

No Private Ballot in Nanaimo
When the first election for Vancouver Island's colonial legislature was held in 1856, men were required to own at least 8 hectares of land in order to vote, and women were not allowed to vote at all. As a result, only one person in the entire riding of Nanaimo was eligible to cast a ballot. In fact, in the whole colony, there were only about 50 qualified voters. (At the time, there were fewer than 500 British residents in Victoria and only about 1000 on the entire island.)

A Double Whammy

In the 1924 provincial election, both Premier John Oliver and the leader of the Opposition, former premier William John Bowser, were defeated for re-election in their own ridings. Though Bowser retired from politics, Oliver went on to win a seat in a by-election. This was the only time in BC history that a premier and a leader of the Opposition were both defeated in the same election.

LET'S PARTY!

Introduction of Party Politics in BC

Before 1903, there were no formal party politics in British Columbia, and most candidates for the Legislative Assembly were elected as individuals rather than as the nominees of any party. However, there were some who ran under various party labels before 1903, including one who called himself a Liberal-Conservative and another who was a Government-Independent. The first to officially list themselves as the nominees of a political party were four individuals who identified themselves as "Labour" and "Workingmen's" candidates in the 1886 election.

Plenty to Choose From
The election with the record number of political parties vying for votes was the 1920 campaign. That year, voters got to choose between the candidates of 15 parties, including the Farmer-Labour-Soldier Party, the Federated Labour Party, the Grand Army of United Veterans, the Independent Soldier Party, the Liberty League of British Columbia, the People's Party-Farmer-Labour, the United Farmers of British Columbia, the Vancouver Ratepayers' Association and the Women's Freedom League. There were also 18 candidates that year calling themselves "independent."

Not Enough Choice?

Since the Great Depression, there have been several political parties that have nominated candidates for the BC Legislative Assembly. Besides the mainstream parties, other political parties have included the Family Choices Party, the Family Coalition, the Financial Justice Party, the Gay Alliance Toward Equality, the Human Race Party, the Libertas of British Columbia, the Libertarian Party, the Natural Law Party, the New Republic, the Rhinoceros Party and the Victory Without Debt Party.

Independence for BC!

The Bloc Québecois and the Parti Québecois are not the only political parties that want to break up Canada. In British Columbia, there is the Bloc British Columbia Party, which seeks independence for BC, and the Western Canada Concept Party, the Western Block Party and the Western Refederation Party, which seek independence or greater autonomy for Canada's four western provinces. However, in the 2005 provincial and the 2006 federal elections, none of the candidates for these parties received more than one percent of the vote in their ridings.

No Sex, Please, We're British (Columbia)

British Columbia's newest political party is the Sex Party. Founded in 2005 by Vancouver lawyer, businessman and sexual politics activist, John Ince, the party describes itself as "the world's first registered political party dedicated exclusively to sex-positive issues" in matters of sexual education and laws regulating prostitution and indecency. In 2005, its three candidates each won less than half of a percent of the vote in their ridings.

THE "WILL" OF THE PEOPLE?

The People's Choice

The only time that a political party won a majority of seats in the BC Legislative Assembly without winning a plurality of the popular vote was in 1996. That year, the New Democratic Party won 39 of the 75 seats, even though they received 37,000 fewer votes than the Liberals (who won only 33 seats).

The People's Choice (Well, Sort of)

Twice a minority government was elected in British Columbia without receiving a plurality of the popular vote. The first time was in 1941, when the provincial Liberals won 21 of the 48 seats in the Legislative Assembly but received 2000 fewer votes than the Commonwealth Cooperative Federation, who won only 14 seats. The second time was in 1952, when the Social Credit Party won 19 of 48 seats but received 28,000 fewer votes than the CCF, who won 18 seats.

POLITICAL FIRSTS

BC's First Female Office Holder

The first woman elected to public office in British Columbia was Maria Grant, who was elected as a school trustee in Victoria in 1895. Active in the temperance and the women's suffrage movements, she later became a minister in the Unity Church.

Madam Judge

The first woman judge in British Columbia was Helen Gregory MacGill, who was appointed to Vancouver's Juvenile Court in 1917. She was also the first woman in the Commonwealth to earn a bachelor of music degree. Her daughter, Elizabeth "Elsie" MacGill, was a distinguished aeronautical engineer who designed the Maple Leaf Trainer aircraft.

Madam Justice

The first woman appointed to the Supreme Court of Canada was BC's Beverly McLachlin in 1989. She was previously a law professor at the University of British Columbia and chief justice of the Supreme Court of BC. In 2000, McLachlin was the first woman to be named chief justice of the federal Supreme Court.

Pathfinders

The first woman to run for, and be elected to, the British Columbia Legislative Assembly was Mary Ellen Smith, who ran as an independent from the riding of Vancouver City in a 1918 by-election. (Women had been given the right to vote in BC only the year before.) Elected to succeed her husband, Smith was re-elected as a provincial Liberal in 1920 and 1924. Also, for eight months in 1921, she was a minister without portfolio in Premier John Oliver's cabinet, making her the first female cabinet minister in the Commonwealth. The first woman elected to the BC legislature who did not succeed her husband in office was Dorothy Steeves, who was chosen to represent North Vancouver in a 1934 by-election.

First Nations Politician Arrives in Victoria!

In 1949, Frank Calder, a Nisga'a, was the first First Nations person elected to the BC legislature. (The prohibition against First Nations voting had been removed only the year before.) He was also the first Canadian of First Nations descent to attend the University of British Columbia. Calder would later play a key role in the Supreme Court's recognition of aboriginal land titles.

Canada's First Indo-Canadian Legislator

The first Indo-Canadian elected to a provincial or federal legislature was Moe Sihota, who was elected to the British Columbia Legislative Assembly in 1986. He later held several cabinet posts under Premier Michael Harcourt.

Canada's First Indo-Canadian Premier

The first (and, so far, only) Indo-Canadian premier in Canada was British Columbia's Ujjal Dosanjh, who served as the premier of BC for 16 months from 2000 to 2001. He was later the federal minister of health under Prime Minister Paul Martin.

Canada's First Chinese Canadian MP

The first Chinese Canadian to run for a seat in either a provincial or federal legislature was Douglas Jung, who was the Progressive Conservative candidate in a 1956 by-election in Vancouver Centre for the British Columbia Legislative Assembly. He lost that election. Named after Douglas Street in Victoria, Jung became the first Chinese Canadian elected to the House of Commons in 1957. He was also the first Chinese Canadian lawyer in British Columbia.

Canada's First Japanese Canadian Politician

The first Japanese Canadian to hold public office in Canada was Masajiro Miyazaki, who was elected an alderman in Lillooet in 1950. An osteopath, Dr. Miyazaki went to the United States in the 1920s to get his degree, because persons of Asian descent were not allowed at the time to attend medical school in British Columbia. Miyazaki had a thriving practice in Vancouver when he was interned with other Japanese Canadians at the camp at Shalalth during World War II. Soon thereafter, the only doctor in nearby Lillooet died, and no other physician could be found who would perform autopsies there, so the provincial constabulary in Lillooet recruited Miyazaki to serve as town coroner. Special wartime permits had to be obtained to allow Miyazaki to live in Lillooet. The doctor's practice quickly expanded to that of general practitioner, including obstetrics and dentistry, with patients as far away as Pemberton, Pavilion, Lytton and the Japanese Canadian community at Taylor Lake. Miyazaki would often have to travel by foot, horseback, rowboat and railway speeder to perform his duties. He also played a key role in the construction of Lillooet's hospital.

GOINGS-ON AT THE LEGISLATIVE ASSEMBLY

Politicians in Birdcages

BC's first government was housed in a series of administrative buildings in Victoria that had been built in 1859 to house the Vancouver Island colonial assembly. With pagoda-like roofs, balconies and brickwork painted various shades of red, the buildings were frequently referred to as the "Birdcages." They were used until the current parliament buildings in Victoria opened in 1898.

Can't Do Business with the Government

Laws prohibiting members of the Legislative Assembly from having any business connections with the provincial government were once quite strict. In 1899, MLA Charles Tisdall was forced to resign his seat because a clerk in his store sold bullets to a police officer. That same year, MLA John Hume had to resign because a policeman stayed overnight at a hotel that Hume owned.

Father and Son

The longest-serving father-and-son legislative team in Canadian history was British Columbia's Ernest and Harold Winch. Both were first elected to the BC Legislative Assembly in 1933 and served together until Ernest's death in 1957. In addition, Ernest was a prominent British Columbia labour leader, while his son was a long-time leader of the provincial Commonwealth Cooperative Federation, twice almost premier of BC and later a 19-year member of the House of Commons.

Knitting Uphill

One day, while the BC Legislative Assembly was in session, the Speaker of the House, Norman Whittaker, noticed that MLA Thomas Uphill was busy at his desk with a ball of wool and a pair of knitting needles. When he inquired what the honourable member was doing, Uphill replied: "Since you, Mr. Speaker, have forbidden members to read newspapers in the House but permit knitting on the floor and in the galleries, I decided to join the BOB." The BOB was the Babies of Britain Club and, as one of its members, Uphill knitted baby garments and sent them to the United Kingdom every month for many years.

Even the Left Was Too Right-Wing

A socialist who was so left wing that he refused to join the Commonwealth Cooperative Federation because it was "too conservative," Thomas Uphill represented the community of Fernie in the BC legislature for 40 years (1920–60). No other provincial or federal legislator in Canada has served for so long. Uphill was also a long-time mayor of Fernie.

The Dickey Birds

In 1902, the members of the loyal opposition in BC's Legislative
Assembly, who were lead by Richard "Dewdney Dick" McBride,
became known as "the Dickey Birds." McBride represented the
riding of Westminster-Dewdney.

First Socialist Premier?

One of the first socialist members of the BC Legislative
Assembly was James Hurst Hawthornthwaite. In fact, some say
that he was the province's first socialist premier.

Hawthornthwaite was elected to the BC Legislative Assembly
from Nanaimo in a 1901 by-election as the candidate of the
Independent Labour Party, and he later joined the Socialist Party
of Canada. Between 1903 and 1907, Premier Richard McBride
and his Conservatives held only 22 seats in the 42-seat legislature, and because of infighting within his own caucus and the
fact that one of his Conservatives was Speaker of the House
(and, thus, could not vote unless there was a tie), McBride often
had trouble getting anything done. McBride came to rely on
Hawthornthwaite so much to prop up his government that the
press frequently called the socialist the "premier-in-fact."

It's My Party and I'll Leave If I Want To!

W.A.C. Bennett entered politics in 1941 as a Conservative. In
1946 and 1950, he tried to become leader of the provincial party,
but was badly trounced each time. Bennett then crossed the aisle
in March 1951 to sit in the Legislative Assembly as an independent. For a while, he considered forming a "people's party based
on genuine free enterprise." Nine months later, he joined the
Social Credit movement. In 1952, Bennett became British
Columbia's first Socred premier. Gordon Wilson had less success. First, he was the leader of the provincial Liberals, but lost
the job in 1993 to Gordon Campbell in a leadership review.

(Party infighting and Wilson's extramarital affair with fellow MLA Judi Tyabji were the cause of his downfall.) Wilson then formed and became leader of the Progressive Democratic Alliance. Much to the surprise of his supporters, Wilson abandoned the PDA in 1999 to join New Democratic Party and Premier Glen Clark's cabinet in 1999. One year later, Wilson ran for the NDP leadership, but lost to Ujjal Dosanjh. When Gordon Campbell and the Liberals won power in their 2001 landslide, Wilson was involuntarily retired from politics. Because of his ever-changing political loyalties, critics called him "Flip" Wilson (after the American comedian).

DID YOU  **KNOW?**

Tommy Douglas may have been, as premier of Saskatchewan (1944–61), the first socialist head of a government in North America, but from 1962 to 1968 and again from 1969 until 1979, he represented first Burnaby and then Nanaimo in the House of Commons. The "Father of Medicare" and one-time federal leader of the New Democratic Party was voted the "Greatest Canadian of All Time" by CBC-TV viewers in 2004.

Thanks for the Holiday!

Robert William Weir Carrall, former Montréal physician and U.S. Army doctor, arrived in British Columbia in 1865 and settled in Barkerville two years later. He got involved in politics, became a major supporter for BC's entry into Confederation, and was appointed to the Senate when the province became part of Canada in 1871. And it was Carrall who introduced the legislation in Parliament making July 1 a national holiday. Originally called Dominion Day, the holiday has been known as Canada Day since 1982.

19TH CENTURY

Look for the Soldier with the Red Sash

The first military (and police) unit in British Columbia was the Victoria Voltigeurs. Organized in 1851 to protect Fort Victoria and provide whatever local policing was needed, the unit consisted mostly of French Canadian and Métis voyageurs who worked for the Hudson's Bay Company. Its members also often accompanied the Royal Navy's expeditions against the First Nations. The Voltigeurs were all volunteers, and their numbers varied from time to time from six to about 30. They used HBC weapons and wore rather non-military-looking uniforms that consisted of a long, sky blue overcoat and a red woollen sash that was worn around the waist. The unit was disbanded when the Royal Engineers arrived in British Columbia in 1858.

Battle in Siberia Leads to Naval Base in BC

Esquimalt's role as a major naval base began with the Crimean War (1853–56). The only major engagement in the Pacific of that war was the British and French naval attack against the Russians at Petropaulovsk in Siberia in 1854. The attack was a disaster, and the British and French wounded were brought to Victoria. However, the small community, which then consisted of only 232 souls, did not have the facilities to care for them. The wounded were taken to San Francisco, but the incident resulted in the establishment of a naval base and the construction of three naval hospital buildings in 1855. Ten years later, Esquimalt became the headquarters of the British North Pacific Squadron.

The Pig War

War almost came to British Columbia in 1859 because of a pig! The Treaty of 1846 between Great Britain and the U.S. divided the Oregon Territory into two halves along the 49th parallel and the Strait of Juan de Fuca, but it was unclear who owned the San Juan Islands between Victoria and present-day Bellingham, Washington. Over the next few years, the Hudson's Bay Company established a fishing station and a sheep farm on San Juan Island, the largest isle in the archipelago, while American farmers also settled there.

Naturally, various disputes over taxes and other matters arose. The whole thing boiled over on June 15, 1859, when an American, Lyman Cutler, shot an HBC pig that was demolishing his garden. The HBC demanded $100 in damages, but Cutler refused to pay. Cutler was then threatened with arrest and a trial in Victoria. General William Harney, commander of the U.S. Military Department of Oregon, heard about the situation and sent Captain George Pickett and 60 men from Fort Bellingham to San Juan Island to protect Cutler and

American interests. In response, Vancouver Island Governor James Douglas sent in British warships and marines. Both sides kept throwing in reinforcements, and by August, it looked as if a real war might start. Fortunately, cooler heads prevailed, and Great Britain and the United States agreed to a joint military occupation of the San Juans until the border dispute was settled. Twelve years later, the matter was submitted to international arbitration, and it was decided that the islands belonged, after all, to the Americans.

Blacks Defend Victoria

One of the first local (non-British) army units in British Columbia was the 45-man Victoria Pioneer Rifles that was organized in 1860. The unit was an essentially all-black volunteer corps with its bandmaster as the only member of European descent. Commonly known as the African Rifles, the unit was mostly self-financed, but Vancouver Island's colonial governor, James Douglas, did offer to supply it with weapons. The Rifles disbanded in 1864 after the unit was snubbed by Douglas' successor, Frederick Seymour (a British bureaucrat who shared the Victorian Age's racial prejudices), and after its members were prohibited from joining the newly formed all-white colonial defence force.

Was the Boer War Really Boring?

Ever since BC joined Confederation in 1871, British Columbians have always fought in Canada's foreign wars. The first such conflict was the South African War (aka the Boer War) that was fought from 1899 to 1902. About 60 volunteers from British Columbia went off to fight, and 24 of them were part of the Royal Canadian Regiment that was involved in the capture of Paardeberg in 1900. Of the British Columbians who went to war, only one—Trooper Timlick from New Westminster—did not come home.

THE WORLD WARS

For King and Country

During both World Wars, more than one out of every 10 British Columbians went off to war! In the Great War, nearly 14 percent, or one out of every seven (55,570 out of a population of only 400,000), left the province to serve in France in the Canadian Expeditionary Force. In World War II, almost 11 percent, or one out of every nine (85,000 out of population of just over 800,000), left home to fight the Axis Powers (Germany, Italy and Japan). In both cases, BC had the highest per capita rate of enlistment of any province in Canada.

DID YOU  KNOW?

Of the almost 62,000 Canadians killed in combat during World War I, 6225 were from British Columbia. And of the approximately 39,000 Canadians killed in World War II, 3423 were from BC.

BC's Japanese Canadian Contribution in World War I

Of the 225 Japanese Canadians who served in the Canadian Expeditionary Force in France during World War I, 196 were from British Columbia. All of them, however, had to go to Alberta to enlist since no British Columbia unit would take them. Of the 196, over one quarter (53) were killed in action and almost half (92) were wounded. The Japanese Canadian War Memorial cenotaph, a marble lantern with an electric "eternal flame" on top, was erected in their honour in Vancouver's Stanley Park in 1920. The flame was extinguished, however, on December 16, 1941, nine days after the Japanese bombed Pearl Harbor, and it was not relit until 1985.

DID YOU  KNOW?

Approximately 300 Chinese Canadians served in the Canadian Expeditionary Force in France during World War I. Most of them were from Vancouver and Victoria, but many had to join battalions from Alberta and Ontario because the units from British Columbia would not take them.

Okanagan First Nations Warriors in France

Although they were second-class citizens in their own country and were even denied the vote, every eligible man between the ages of 20 and 35 in British Columbia's Okanagan Head of the Lake First Nations band enlisted and fought in France during World War I.

BC's VC Winners

The Victoria Cross, the highest decoration for bravery in the Commonwealth, has been awarded over the years to 20 soldiers, sailors and aviators who were from BC or connected to a British Columbia military unit. (Since 1993, Canada has had its own version of the Victoria Cross.) Fifteen of the 70 Canadians who earned the Victoria Cross in World War I were from British Columbia, as were five of the 16 Canadians who won it in World War II.

Receiving the VC for Non-Violent Acts

Most recipients of the Victoria Cross are awarded the medal for an act of valour that involves the killing of enemy soldiers. But two BC recipients of the award from World War I won the VC for non-violent acts. Piper James Richardson was posthumously awarded the Victoria Cross for playing his bagpipes at Regina Trench at the Battle of the Somme in 1916, while in full view of the Germans, in order to rally his fellow soldiers for an attack. Shortly afterwards, while taking the wounded and some prisoners back to Allied lines, Richardson returned to the battlefield to retrieve his pipes and disappeared, never to be seen again. A year later, Private Michael O'Rourke, a unarmed stretcher bearer, saved many lives over three days and nights by bringing the wounded to safety at Hill 17 in northern France. In doing so, O'Rourke often exposed himself to German shelling, snipers and machine-gun fire. At times, he was even buried by the dirt that was kicked up by exploding enemy shells. O'Rourke went on to become a noted labour activist.

German Fleet Threatens British Columbia!

Shortly after World War I began in 1914, the German East Asiatic Squadron, consisting of five battle cruisers under the command of Vice-Admiral Graf Maximilian von Spee, left its home base at Tsingtao, China, and sailed into the Pacific Ocean, where it attacked Allied shipping. At the time, the only naval vessel protecting British Columbia was a training cruiser, the HMCS *Rainbow*, and there were fears of an imminent German attack on BC's coast and Vancouver. Two other smaller vessels, the HMS *Algerine* and the HMS *Shearwater*, were quickly brought up north from Mexican waters, and two submarines, the *CC1* and the *CC2*, were purchased right off the docks in Seattle. Furthermore, improvised crews were put together, privately owned auxiliary boats were pressed into service and guns were installed at Point Grey and Point Atkinson. Still, they would have been no match for the German fleet that sank two British cruisers off the coast of Chile at the Battle of Coronel on November 1, 1914. It wasn't until Spee's fleet was destroyed a month later at the Battle of the Falkland Islands that British Columbians breathed a sigh of relief.

DID YOU KNOW?

When rumours reached British Columbia just before the beginning of World War I in August 1914 that German destroyers were heading north from California, the residents of Victoria naturally panicked. Some even bought plots at the Ross Bay Cemetery for use as bomb shelters.

The British Columbia Navy

Canada's only provincial navy existed for merely three days and consisted of just two submarines—and they had no torpedoes! On August 3, 1914, two German cruisers were allegedly seen off Washington State's Cape Flattery. The rumours proved false, but the next day, only hours before war was declared between Germany and the British Empire (of which Canada was still a part), BC Premier Richard McBride authorized $1.15 million for the purchase of two Chilean submarines that were being built in Seattle.

Originally called the *Antofagasta* and the *Iquique*, the submarines were renamed the *CC1* and the *CC2*; the first "C" stood for "Canadian" and the second for the vessels' resemblance to Britain's "C" class subs. Their crews were all volunteers and included veterans of the Royal Navy as well as sailors who had never before seen a submarine.

The presence of the submarines in BC's waters was widely advertised to hopefully deter a German attack in case any spies were listening; indeed, fear was the subs' only weapon because they lacked torpedoes (a fact that was *not* told to the public). The *CC1* and the *CC2* were quickly transferred to the Royal Canadian Navy and spent three peaceful years cruising and training off the BC coast before they were transferred to Halifax. While sailing to the Atlantic, the submarines became the first Canadian naval vessels to transit the Panama Canal.

The Japanese Attack British Columbia!
On June 20, 1942, for about 40 minutes, the Japanese submarine *I-26* fired between 25 and 30 shells at the lighthouse and wireless station at Estevan Point near Tofino. That same day, another submarine attacked a British freighter, the SS *Camosun*, off Washington's coast, and on June 21, a Japanese sub shelled Fort Stevens in Oregon.

Although there were no casualties and little damage, the incident at Estevan Point did heighten fears of a major Japanese attack on British Columbia. It also effectively put a halt to all nighttime shipping along BC's coast for the rest of the war because, as a result of the attack, the lights of all the outer coastal stations were turned off to prevent enemy subs from using the lighthouses as points of reference at night. The shelling of Estevan Point was the first attack on Canadian soil since the War of 1812.

Or Was It the Americans?

Some historians claim that it wasn't the Japanese who attacked Estevan Point in 1942, but the Americans. According to the theory, the shelling of the lighthouse was part of a secret plan to force the Canadian federal government to enact conscription. (Until 1942, all soldiers and sailors fighting for Canada during World War II were volunteers.) If true, it's a funny way to treat your neighbour and ally. An unexploded Japanese shell from the *I-26* was discovered at Estevan Point in 1973, but doubters still insist that it was the Americans who attacked.

Here Come the Gumboats!

The Fishermen's Reserve, better known as the "Gumboat Navy," wasn't your typical naval unit. Instead, it consisted of recruits who allowed their fishing boats to be outfitted with guns and equipment for the purpose of patrolling the BC coast during World War II. Organized in 1939, at one time 42 vessels and almost 1000 men were involved, but the unit was disbanded in 1944 after the fear of a Japanese invasion subsided.

Vancouver Attacked by Fishing Boats!

During World War II, searchlights, gun batteries, observation posts and military camps were installed and constructed at various points surrounding Burrard Inlet for the defence of Vancouver. There were also numerous regulations that all incoming vessels had to follow when entering the bay, and failure to do so was considered a "hostile act," which subjected the ship to battery fire.

In 1942, a fishing boat, the *Georgie*, had no radio gear and ignored all the rules. Not only was a non-explosive warning shot fired into the water in front of the ship to stop it, but its captain later received a bill for $42.50 for the cost of the round!

That same year, another fishing boat ignored the wartime restrictions as it entered Burrard Inlet. A warning shot was fired, but instead of plunging into the water, the non-explosive round skipped across the surface and put a big hole into the *Fort Rae*, a new 8700-tonne freighter then undergoing speed trials in nearby English Bay. To prevent its sinking, the crew of the *Fort Rae* had to beach the ship near Lions' Gate Bridge.

WAR HEROES AND TRAITORS

Top Ace!

Of the 27 Allied aces who shot down 30 or more enemy planes during World War I, BC's Lieutenant Colonel Raymond Collishaw, with 60 aircraft and eight observation balloon kills, was the third-highest-scoring Allied fighter pilot of the war. (Some historians credit him with 81 kills, which would make him the greatest ace of the war.) The commander of the famous Black Flight of the Royal Naval Air Service's Number 10 Naval Squadron, Collishaw was also the first Allied pilot to shoot down six enemy planes in a single day. Not bad for an ex-sailor who was rejected three times for the air service and had to pay for his own flying lessons.

The School Teacher–General

BC's Arthur Currie was one of the most successful Allied generals of World War I and possibly the greatest in Canadian history. The first Canadian to command the Canadian Expeditionary Force in France, he was responsible for the victory at Vimy Ridge (1917) and led the Canadians at Passchendaele (1917) and the Battle of Amiens (1918).

Some historians believe that, had World War I lasted much longer, Currie would have replaced British General Douglas Haig as the commander in chief of the British Imperial forces on the Western Front. Ironically, Currie was not a professional soldier, but a schoolteacher, insurance salesman and realtor from Vancouver Island, whose only military experience before the war had been as a part-time officer in the local militia.

General Currie, Embezzler

General Arthur Currie may be one of Canada's greatest military heroes, but he was also a crook. Just before World War I began in 1914, Currie embezzled $10,000 (money that was supposed to be spent on uniforms) from his own militia unit, the 5th BC Garrison of Artillery. He avoided criminal prosecution only because a group of friends took a collection and paid back the money. The whole affair came to light in 1917 after Currie's great victory at Vimy Ridge. Rather than disgrace a war hero, Prime Minister Robert Borden had the matter dropped.

Kid General

Vancouver-native Bertram Hoffmeister became the youngest Canadian divisional commander in World War II when he was promoted to major general and placed in charge of the 5th Canadian Armoured Division in 1944 at the tender age of 36. He later commanded the division in its successful attack against the Germans' Gothic Line in Italy and was chosen to lead Canada's troops in the invasion of Japan (an invasion that, fortunately, never happened).

BC's Traitor

The nickname "Kamloops Kid" is not one of affection. Kanao Inouye was the son of a Japanese Canadian who served in the Canadian Army during World War I. He was born and raised in Kamloops, but the 19-year-old went to Japan with his mother in 1935 and never returned. Inouye was an interpreter at a Japanese POW camp and worked for the Japanese secret service during World War II. Seething with hatred because of the racism he suffered as a boy, the "Kamloops Kid" brutalized the Allied prisoners under his control and murdered at least three of them. Still a Canadian citizen, Inouye was tried for treason after the war and executed.

Hammy

British Columbian Lieutenant Robert "Hammy" Gray was the last Canadian to die in action in World War II. On August 9, 1945, the same day that the atomic bomb was dropped on Nagasaki, the 28-year-old navy pilot led his squadron on an attack against a Japanese destroyer, the *Amakusa*, in Onagawa Bay at Honshu, Japan. With his Corsair hit by enemy shells and on fire, with only one bomb left, and despite heavy fire from enemy shore batteries as well as from his target and four other ships, Gray pressed on and scored a direct hit, sinking the destroyer before his own plane crashed into the water. He didn't try to bail out, and his body was never recovered. For his bravery, Gray was awarded the Victoria Cross.

For Whom the Bell Tolls

Approximately 400 British Columbians, more than one-fourth of the 1448 Canadians who fought against General Francisco Franco and the fascists during the Spanish Civil War (1936–39), served with the Mackenzie-Papineau Battalion. Known as the "Mac-Paps," the battalion was one of the International Brigades that consisted of volunteers from 53 countries who, at their own expense, went to Spain to support its democratically elected government against Franco and troops from Nazi Germany and Italy.

Fighting in Spain was bitter (a 50 percent casualty rate, and the fascists did not take prisoners). In addition, the Canadian government not only gave the Mac-Paps the cold shoulder, but Parliament enacted a law in 1937 making it illegal for Canadians to serve in the International Brigades. After years of being ignored, a monument was finally erected in the Mac-Paps' honour in Victoria in 2000.

British Columbians in Korea

Canada's first casualty in the Korean War was RSM James Wood from Vancouver, who was accidentally killed in 1951 when a land mine exploded during a training exercise. Although Wood was not among them, 22 British Columbians were killed in action during that war.

BC's Korean War Hero

As its lieutenant colonel, British Columbia's James R. Stone led the 2nd Battalion of the Princess Patricia's Canadian Light Infantry during the Korean War. Under his command, the 800-man battalion, while greatly outnumbered and surrounded on three sides by 6000 Chinese and North Korean troops, stopped a major Communist offensive at Kapyong in 1951 and prevented the near-certain capture of Seoul. As a result of this action, the battalion was the only Canadian unit during the war to receive the U.S. Presidential Citation.

THE FIRST ASIANS IN BRITISH COLUMBIA

Japanese Shipwreck Survivors in BC

In 1833, two Japanese sailors were shipwrecked off the Queen Charlotte Islands, rescued by the Hudson's Bay Company and taken to England. This was the first recorded Japanese shipwreck off BC's coast. Over the following years, other Japanese shipwreck survivors either made it back to Japan, where they faced criminal prosecution (since it was illegal at the time for Japanese citizens to travel to foreign countries) or stayed in BC and lived with (and perhaps even assimilated into) the local First Nations' population.

The First Japanese Immigrant to Canada

The first Japanese person who voluntarily immigrated to Canada was Manzo Nagano, a 19-year-old (some sources say 22-year-old) carpenter's apprentice from Nagasaki who stowed away on a British vessel in Yokohama and jumped ship in New Westminster in 1877. He eventually ended up in Victoria, where he worked at a Japanese-financed lumber mill and later owned a hotel and a store. Nagano also made a fortune exporting BC pickled salmon to his native country.

First Chinese Immigrants to Canada

The first Chinese to arrive in Canada were the approximately 120 artisans who arrived at Nootka Sound on British fur-trading vessels in 1788–89. They were brought there by fur-trader John Meares to construct a trading post and to settle in a colony near the First Nations summer village of Yuquot. They also helped build the first sailing vessel launched on the BC coast, the *North West America*.

Would Have Been a Lawyer But For...

Port Douglas native Won Alexander Cumyow was the first person of Chinese descent to be born in Canada. A BC high school graduate and a student of law, he was not allowed to become an attorney because of his Asian ancestry and was employed instead as a court and police interpreter. Cumyow voted in the 1890 provincial election but had to wait 57 years before he could cast his second ballot. In the meantime, Canadian citizens of Chinese descent were denied the vote in British Columbia. Cumyow was the only Chinese Canadian to vote in BC both before and after the disenfranchisement. According to some, he was also the first Chinese Canadian to vote in the 1949 federal election.

First Sikh Immigrants to Canada

The first Sikhs to come to Canada were not immigrants, but Punjabi soldiers of the Sikh Lancers and Infantry Regiment who visited Vancouver in 1897. They were on their way back to their army base in Hong Kong after taking part in Queen Victoria's Diamond Jubilee in London, England. Apparently, the troops liked what they saw of BC and spread the word, because the first Sikh immigrants from India arrived and settled in Vancouver and Victoria just two years later. By 1901, there were 258 Sikhs living in British Columbia.

Calls for an All-White Canada

In 1907, Henry Herbert Stevens, Vancouver alderman, ardent moralist and leader of the Asiatic Exclusion League, publicly stated: "We contend that the destiny of Canada is best left in the hands of the Anglo-Saxon race and are 'unalterably and irrevocably' opposed to any move which threatens in the slightest degree this position." Stevens then continued: "As far as Canada is concerned, it shall remain white, and our doors shall be closed to the Hindoos [sic] as well as to other Orientals." These views were not abhorrent to most British Columbians or Canadians at the time; in fact, Stevens was elected from Vancouver in 1911 to the first of five terms in the House of Commons and would serve in the cabinet of Prime Ministers Arthur Meighen and R.B. Bennett.

Ship Them Out of Here!

By 1908, there were about 5000 Sikhs in Canada, virtually all of whom were living in British Columbia. The province's population at the time was over 300,000, and one wouldn't assume that the small number of Sikhs would have posed a threat to anyone, but the majority in BC thought otherwise. The year before, all natives of India were denied the vote in BC (even though they were British subjects) unless their parents were of European descent. Public works contracts specified that Sikhs could not be hired.

In response to public pressure from BC, the federal government adopted a regulation requiring all immigrants who arrived by ship to have travelled directly to Canada without their vessel stopping off at any port along the way. Since there was no direct passage at the time between India and Canada, this effectively stopped all Sikh immigration. And in 1908, there was an effort to deport all Sikhs in Canada to the colony of British Honduras (now the country of Belize) in order to "keep Canada white." Ottawa even paid two Sikh leaders to visit the Central American colony, but when the two reported back about the poor economic and living conditions there, the Sikhs in BC refused to go, and the deportation idea died. Still, the message was clear. In 1911, the Sikh population in British Columbia was 2342 (less than half that of 1908), and by 1918, there were only about 700 left. It wasn't until the wives and minor children of the Sikhs who were already in BC were allowed to immigrate to Canada in 1919 that the numbers started rising again.

Floating Ghetto and Riots in Vancouver Harbour

In 1914, a wealthy Sikh businessman, Gurdit Singh Sarhali, chartered the Japanese steamer, the *Komagata Maru*, for $66,000 for the purpose of challenging the regulations that were stopping Sikh immigration. The ship sailed on April 4 and arrived at Vancouver's Burrard Inlet on May 23 with 376 passengers. However, except for 22 individuals who were returning to Canada, no one was allowed to disembark. Local residents were not allowed to approach the *Komagata Maru*, officials did not allow the vessel's provisions to be replenished, nor was any communication permitted between ship and shore. For two months the conditions on the ship deteriorated as the summer heat bore down on the vessel, and food and water became scarce. On June 28, a court upheld the government's regulations and ordered the *Komagata Maru* to leave, but its passengers refused to go. By July 17, conditions were so bad that the passengers on the *Komagata Maru* rioted and took over the ship. One hundred and twenty-five armed police officers and 25 immigration officers (who were ex-soldiers) tried to board the ship and return control to the ship's captain but were turned back with bricks, coal and wooden spears. The federal government then brought in an eight-gun naval cruiser, the HMCS *Rainbow*, with troops on her deck and orders to sink the *Komagata Maru* if it did not leave. On July 23, the *Komagata Maru* was escorted out to sea while thousands of Vancouver residents cheered from the shores.

Hero in World War I, But "Enemy Alien" in World War II
Sergeant Masumi Mitsui of Port Coquitlam was among 196 BC Japanese Canadians who fought in France with the Canadian Expeditionary Force during World War I. A hero of Vimy Ridge, Mitsui came home with the Military Medal (one of the British Empire's highest military decorations). But during World War II, after Canada and Japan went to war, Mitsui and his wife and children were declared "enemy aliens" and were shipped off to an internment camp at Greenwood, BC. His home, farm and possessions were confiscated and sold off.

EARLY BLACK HISTORY IN BC

The Promised Land

The first blacks in British Columbia arrived from San Francisco in 1858. Although California was a "free" state, racism was rampant. At the urging of Governor James Douglas of Vancouver Island, about 400 black families (over 1000 people) left their homes and arrived at Esquimalt on April 25, 1858, on board the *Commodore*, the same vessel that had brought the first gold miners to Victoria just a month before. Most settled in or near Victoria, a number went to Saltspring Island and a few went to the BC mainland to seek their fortune in the Fraser River Gold Rush.

Celebrating Freedom

During their first few years in British Columbia, blacks in Victoria celebrated the end of slavery in the West Indies on every August 1. The ceremonies included the closing for the day of all black-owned businesses and a parade through the city's streets to Cadboro Bay, where up to 200 people would feast at a picnic. After Abraham Lincoln freed the slaves in the United States in 1863, the holiday turned into a celebration of the end of slavery in America.

Early Black Leader in BC

Mifflin Wistar Gibbs may have been the first black municipal judge elected in the United States, but before that he played a major role in British Columbia politics. A businessman and publisher from California, he was one of the blacks who immigrated to Victoria in 1858 to escape racism.

Gibbs became a successful merchant by selling supplies to miners who were on their way to the Fraser River Gold Rush and then by opening and operating the first general store in BC that was not run by the Hudson's Bay Company. Gibbs helped organize the Victoria Pioneer Rifles and, in 1866, was elected to Victoria's city council. He even served for a time as acting mayor. In 1868, he was a delegate to the Yale Convention, a meeting of 26 civic leaders from around British Columbia that played a key role in the colony's eventual entry into Confederation. Gibbs returned to the United States in 1869, where he later served as a judge, diplomat and banker.

THE DUNSMUIRS:
COAL KINGS OF
VANCOUVER ISLAND

Immigrant Makes Good

Robert Dunsmuir was a Scottish immigrant who made a fortune in coal mining and other businesses. By 1883, he was the richest man in British Columbia, owning one-fifth of Vancouver Island!

If You've Got It, Flaunt It!

To celebrate his financial success, in 1887, Robert Dunsmuir ordered the construction of a castle in Victoria. Craigdarroch, also known as Dunsmuir Castle, was up to that time the most expensive residence ever built in western Canada. But Dunsmuir never lived there; he died before it was completed. Soon after the death of Dunsmuir's wife in 1908, the home was sold, and it later served as a military hospital and as the site of Victoria College (now the University of Victoria). Former student Pierre Berton's autograph can still be seen carved on the wall of the building's Dogwood Room. Today, the castle is a popular tourist attraction.

A Unique "Common Working Man"

Upon Robert Dunsmuir's death, his son, James, became the richest person in BC. Still, the younger Dunsmuir described himself as a "common working man." When he said this, he lived in a 50-room custom-made medieval castle on 260 hectares in Esquimalt that had its own dairy and slaughterhouse. (The castle, called Hatley Castle, is now the university administration building at Royal Roads University.) Dunsmuir also had a 66-metre yacht with a dining room that could seat 24 and his own private fishing lodge. And he owned another great mansion, Burleith, in Victoria, which burned down in 1931. Not bad for a "common working man."

Champion of Asian Rights?

In the early 1900s, when anti-Asian feelings were running high in British Columbia, James Dunsmuir went to court to fight government restrictions against the hiring of Chinese and Japanese workers. His motives, however, were not purely altruistic. Dunsmuir was the largest employer of Asian labour in the province, and at the time, the Chinese and Japanese were willing to work for much lower wages than their white counterparts. In addition, Dunsmuir paid his lawyers by docking the wages of his Asian employees.

OUTLAWS AND LAWMEN

The Grey Fox

The American outlaw Bill Miner spent virtually his entire adult
life behind bars before he came to BC's Nicola Valley in 1904.
While living there for two years as a gentleman rancher named
George Edwards, he took the time to hold up two Canadian
Pacific Railway trains. Miner and his accomplices got away on
September 10, 1904, with $7000 in gold and cash plus a fortune
in bonds from the robbery near Mission. It was BC's first train
robbery. However, the second robbery, which occurred outside
Kamloops on May 8, 1906, netted Miner and his friends only
$15 and a bottle of liver pills. (Miner was also involved in a 1905
train robbery north of Seattle that netted him about $35,000.)
Miner was caught near Douglas Lake shortly after the Kamloops
robbery. Tried and sentenced to life in prison, he soon escaped
from the New Westminster Penitentiary, some believe with the

collusion of the CPR in exchange for the location of the stolen bonds. Miner returned to the United States and eventually died in a Georgia prison.

DID YOU KNOW?

Despite his profession, Bill Miner was a hero to many British Columbians because of his enormous charm and the fact that he stole from the unpopular CPR. Known as the "Gentleman Bandit" because of his polite ways, Miner is credited with inventing the phrase "Hands up!"

Murderer Dangles Over His Victim

Dr. Max William Fifer was a San Francisco doctor who joined the Fraser River Gold Rush in 1858. He became prominent in local politics and was soon elected to Yale's town council. But in 1861, a fellow miner, Robert Wall, murdered Fifer. Wall's motive was revenge: a drunk had just told him that the wolfs-bane that Fifer prescribed for a medical problem had made Wall impotent. Ironically, Wall's gallows were built directly over Fifer's grave so that, when Wall was hanged, his feet dangled just a few feet in the air above his victim's remains.

Big John

Wherever the 191-centimetre-tall, 136-kilogram "Big John" Kirkup served as a lawman in the mining towns of BC, he often was literally "the law" and few cases ever reached a judge or jury. For instance, on a visit to Rossland, Kirkup learned of a squatter who had built a shack near the local creek, thereby endangering the community's water supply. After confronting the vagrant, who adamantly stood his ground, Kirkup simply put his shoulder to the shack, "put his back into it" and pushed the entire structure into the water.

Friendly Persuasion

Jack Lucy, a famous gunfighter from Idaho, once decided to visit Rossland. And Sheriff "Big John" Kirkup met him on the outskirts of the town. Kirkup simply put his hand on the gunman's shoulder, questioned Lucy as to why he was there and subtly suggested that Lucy head back to the United States. As the gunfighter kept giving answers that Kirkup did not want to hear, the sheriff continued to tighten his grip. It didn't take too long for Lucy to get the message, turn around and go back to Idaho.

DID YOU  **KNOW?**

In 1911, a group of safecrackers tunnelled into the Bank of Montreal branch in New Westminster and came out with approximately $250,000—that would be over $3 million today. It was the largest bank robbery in North America up to that time.

Women Don't Belong in the Courtroom!

Mabel French had to overcome tremendous obstacles to become British Columbia's first woman lawyer—and all because she was not a "person." In 1905, French became the first woman to graduate from the law program at King's College in New Brunswick (and with honours no less!), but the law society there refused to admit her because French was not a "person" according to the law governing the province's legal profession. The New Brunswick Supreme Court agreed, so French arranged to be sued by her creditors in order to argue that, because she was not a "person," she was not responsible for her debts.

French ended up having to pay her bills, but her trial focused public attention on the absurdity of the situation, and the law was changed in 1907 to allow women to become lawyers. French moved to Vancouver three years later and tried to join a local law firm but had to go through the hoops all over again. Like their Maritime counterparts, the BC Law Society and Court of Appeal ruled that French could not practise law because she was not a "person." However, one of the attorneys in her prospective firm was a friend of Evelyn Farris, a prominent social activist and wife of Vancouver's crown prosecutor, John Wallace Farris. Mrs. Farris immediately started a campaign on French's behalf. Under public pressure, the BC government enacted legislation to remove the prohibition against women practising law, and Mabel French was admitted to the British Columbia bar in 1912.

Wild West Gunfight in New Hazelton

Right out of the pages of Dodge City and Tombstone, Canada's only Wild West–style shootout occurred in New Hazelton on April 7, 1914, when seven bank robbers found themselves in a raging gun battle with the town's residents. Four men had robbed the community's Union Bank of $18,000 five months earlier but had gotten away, and the money was never recovered.

The robbery was part of a crime wave sweeping through BC's northern Interior, and the townsfolk were furious. And it didn't help when the local police chief and his deputy, while tracking the suspects, killed an innocent man who ignored their order to halt. (Perhaps because he was only a "half-breed" while the deceased was white, the deputy who fired the fatal shot was quickly tried, convicted of murder and sent to prison.) So when seven men attempted another theft at the same bank, the citizenry did not wait for the police. Guns and rifles were drawn, and a two-minute gunfight in the streets ensued between the bandits and the local residents. (Some sources say that it was the thieves from the previous robbery plus three new cohorts.) Over 200 shots were fired, and even women dodged flying bullets to bring more cartridges to their men when the ammunition ran out.

Three of the bank robbers were killed in the shootout, and three others were wounded and led off to jail. Only one local resident, a bank teller, was wounded. The seventh man got away but was finally caught nine years later. The four survivors turned out to be Russian immigrants, and all spent 20 years in the New Westminster Penitentiary for attempted bank robbery before being deported to their home country. However, most of the $1400 stolen in the second theft was never found.

Brother XII

Ever hear of Edward Arthur Wilson? No? Well, how about
Brother XII? Wilson was a former bank clerk, Royal Navy veteran and BC coastal steamer captain. In 1924, he experienced
some mystical visions that he interpreted as messages from powerful Egyptian deities and, during the next year, would go into
trances and write a book that was "dictated" to him by a spiritual
being. Renaming himself "Brother XII" or the "Twelfth Brother
of the Great White Lodge," Wilson predicted an apocalypse that
would be followed by an age of enlightenment. At one point, he
claimed to be the reincarnation of the Egyptian god Osiris.
Brother XII and his 2000 followers, many of whom were quite
wealthy, established colonies at Cedar-by-the-Sea near Nanaimo
and later on nearby Valdez and De Courcy Islands. However, his
increasingly erratic and violent behaviour, dictatorial manners
and financial and sexual scandals resulted in Brother XII's downfall. In 1932, Wilson disappeared with his mistress and four
boxes of gold coins that weighed a half a tonne and had a worth
of approximately $400,000. He supposedly died in Switzerland
two years later, but many believe that his death was faked—and
the money was never found.

Brother of Brother XII

BC's cult leader Brother XII had a younger brother, Herbert
Emerson Wilson, the self-proclaimed "King of the Safecrackers."
Herbert Wilson was a decorated Boer War veteran and Baptist-
minister-turned-master-safecracker who blew up 65 safes across
the United States between 1917 and 1923. He stole an estimated
$16 million before getting caught and spending 12 years in San
Quentin Prison. Wilson was deported to Canada upon his
release in 1935, and then he later spent six years in a Canadian
prison for a scam that he always insisted he had no part of. Once
the "King" was finally free, he retired from his life of crime,
moved to Vancouver. At one time, there was even talk of Tony
Curtis portraying him in a movie.

BC's Most Elusive Fugitive

The son of a hereditary Gitxsan chief, Simon Gunanoot (also spelled Gun-An-Noot) was a successful trapper, rancher and store merchant. The strong, 183-centimetre-tall man could travel 64 kilometres on foot over rough terrain in a single day and, because of his strength and endurance, was something of a celebrity in the Hazelton area. He also became British Columbia's most famous fugitive.

In 1906, Gunanoot got into a barroom fight with a Hazelton dockworker named Alex McIntosh, and witnesses heard him threaten McIntosh's life. A few hours later, McIntosh and another man, Max Leclair, were found dead. Besides the threats, there was no evidence against Gunanoot and his brother-in-law, Peter Hi-maden (who was also accused of the murders). However, rather than take their chances with an all-white jury (First Nations people were not yet allowed to sit on juries), the two men fled with their large families into the BC wilderness.

For nearly 13 years, Gunanoot and Hi-maden eluded the provincial police, RCMP, bounty hunters and Pinkerton detectives, becoming national legends in the process. Meanwhile, the fugitives lived off the land, sold furs whenever they could and travelled from Bear Lake to Telegraph Creek and McDames. Hundreds of thousands of hours and over $100,000 were spent trying to find them, making it the most expensive manhunt in BC's history up to that time, but it was all for naught; they never caught Gunanoot or Hi-maden.

Gunanoot gave himself up in 1918. Represented by Canada's best criminal defence lawyer, Stuart Henderson of Victoria, Gunanoot was acquitted of murder; it took the jury only 13 minutes to reach its verdict. Hi-maden gave himself up in 1920, and the charges against him were dropped for lack of evidence.

DID YOU  **KNOW?**

Though Simon Gunanoot turned himself into the authorities in 1918, he had delayed his surrender and remained in the BC wilderness for a few extra months. The reason? Gunanoot wanted to pay his defence lawyer in cash and needed another season in the mountains to trap and collect enough furs to pay his attorney's fee.

Prosecutor "Gets" Gunanoot in the End

For most of the investigation's 13 years, BC Attorney General William Bowser was in charge of the pursuit of Simon Gunanoot in the British Columbia wilderness. Bowser's efforts were not successful. Gunanoot was never apprehended, but he turned himself in and was acquitted of the charges in 1918. Gunanoot died 15 years later and is buried beside his father. His grave lies in a beautiful setting that overlooks a remote lake in the mountains near Stewart. The name of that body of water: Bowser Lake. It's named after the attorney general who tried so hard to capture Gunanoot.

The Clarence Darrow of British Columbia

When he successfully represented the famous Simon Gunanoot against murder charges in 1918, Stuart Henderson, of Ashcroft and later Victoria, was already regarded as the best criminal defence lawyer in Canada. A former federal government lawyer and one-time member of the BC Legislative Assembly, only five of the 50 men that he represented in murder cases were convicted.

This did not endear Henderson to either the prosecutors or the government. Neither did the fact that Henderson was well known for his willingness to represent defendants who were aboriginal. Attorney General William Bowser (no lover of First Nations rights) considered Henderson to be an "agitator" who aimed to "baffle the administration of justice in the Province." Among First Nations peoples, however, Henderson was called "Great White Friend."

Murder Mystery

BC's most famous unsolved murder case is that of 22-year-old Janet Smith. The Scottish handmaid was found dead in 1924 at the Shaughnessy Heights mansion of her employer, World War I hero and Vancouver pharmaceutical drug merchant Frederick Turner. She was discovered with a bullet hole above her right eye and a .45-calibre revolver at her side.

The case had everything, including allegations of sex, drugs and domestic violence among the city's affluent elite, as well as charges of political interference in the investigation and a police cover-up. No arrests were ever made, but in 1925, the Chinese houseboy who found the body, Wong Foon Sing, was kidnapped by a mob dressed in the white sheets of the Ku Klux Klan. For six weeks, Wong was shackled to the floor of a room, beaten and threatened with death by his captors in an attempt to get him to confess or reveal who committed the murder. The night of his release, police found a delirious Wong walking along a street. He was taken into custody and charged with Smith's murder.

The accusation was absurd, and Wong was released for lack of evidence. But after six more weeks, Point Grey's reeve (i.e., mayor), police chief and four constables, as well as three private detectives who worked for the city of Point Grey, were arrested for Wong's kidnapping! Surprisingly, the men did not deny the charges at their trial, but claimed that they had been working under orders from BC Attorney General Alexander Manson. Manson refuted the charges, but they ruined his chances of becoming premier. Amazingly, while the three detectives were convicted and went to prison, the other six were acquitted and set free.

Wong returned to China in 1926, and the Smith case was officially closed. The murder has never been solved.

The Klan in British Columbia

Although normally associated with the American South, the white supremacist Ku Klux Klan was active in British Columbia in the late 1920s and early 1930s. A local chapter opened in Vancouver in 1925 at a Shaughnessy Heights mansion called Glen Brae, and within two years, the KKK claimed 8000 members in the city and another 5000 elsewhere in the province. Since not many blacks lived in BC at the time, the organization focused on the province's Asian population and called for a halt to Asian immigration and the government seizure of property owned by Canadians of Asian descent. Eventually, Vancouver passed a bylaw making it illegal to wear a mask in public, and that, along with the theft of the organization's funds by its founder, led to the Klan's disappearance from British Columbia. There was a brief KKK revival in BC in the 1980s, but fortunately it didn't go anywhere and did not last very long.

From Labour Activist to Police Spy

Agent 10—the name sounds like BC's version of Maxwell Smart (Agent 99) or James Bond (007). But Robert Gosden, aka Agent 10, was a famous BC labour activist in the early 20th century who openly advocated violence and revolution in support of the labour cause. He helped organize the Prince Rupert Industrial Association, which was affiliated with the famous militant union, the Industrial Workers of the World (better known as the Wobblies), and was the president of the Miners' Liberation League. He even once warned Premier Richard McBride and Attorney General William John Bowser that they could be murdered if they did not release a group of jailed miners. But by 1919, Gosden had become a spy for the Royal Canadian Mounted Police.

No one knows for sure why he did it, but as Agent 10, Gosden reported on the goings-on of the 1919 Western Labour Conference that lead to the One Big Union, and he continued spying on the activities of the labour movement for a few years after that. He even urged the government to kidnap key labour leaders and have them "disappear" in order to spread fear and terror among his fellow activists. But by the early 1920s, Gosden had served his purpose, and the Mounties fired him.

Wouldn't Dad be Proud?

Allan (or Allen), Charley and Archie McLean were the sons of Donald McLean, a prominent Hudson's Bay Company fur trader who once ran the company post at Fort Kamloops. During the worldwide depression of 1877, with their father dead, the gold rush over and jobs scarce in the Kamloops area, the three boys (aged 14 to 22) joined a local outlaw, Alexander Hare, and turned to stealing.

For the next two years, the McLean Gang stole horses, ammunition, food and clothing in the Nicola Valley. On December 8, 1879, five days after the McLeans stole a horse, BC Provincial Policeman John Ussher and three others surprised the McLeans and Hare. In one of the most famous gunfights in BC history, shots were fired and Ussher was killed. The gang then fled, killing another man and stealing from others as they attempted to elude a posse. The four tried to hide out at a cabin on Douglas Lake, but were soon surrounded by 70 men. On December 13, hungry, thirsty, tired and hopelessly outnumbered, the McLeans and Hare surrendered.

Convicted twice of murder (the first verdicts were thrown out on a technicality), the four were hanged together on January 31, 1881, at the penitentiary in New Westminster. Archie, aged 18 at the time, was the youngest person executed in BC history. Allan's son, George, later became a Canadian hero at the Battle of Vimy Ridge in World War I.

Cross-Dressing at Sea!

Jemmy Jones was a sea captain who regularly sailed between Puget Sound and Vancouver Island. Jailed in Victoria in 1865 for not paying his debts, Jones escaped and crossed the Juan de Fuca Strait in a canoe (while dressed as a woman!) in order to steal his own ship from his creditors. Jones then sailed the vessel up the Georgia Strait, around the northern tip of Vancouver Island and then south to Mexico and freedom. He later sold the boat, paid his debts and returned to British Columbia to resume his profession. Jemmy Jones Island in Baynes Channel is named after him.

THE "HANGING JUDGE"
AND OTHER MONIKERED JURISTS

The Hanging Judge?

Matthew Begbie, a jurist in British Columbia from 1858 until 1894, is known today as the "Hanging Judge," though he was never called that while he was alive. The nickname arose only years after his death, when writers attempted to romanticize the province's Gold Rush days. In addition, while tough in his administration of the criminal law, Begbie never participated in, or even watched, the hanging of anyone condemned in his court. Indeed, he was actually repulsed by the idea of taking human life, even if it was that of a murderer. From 1858 to 1871, when Begbie alone tried most of the capital cases in BC's mainland, he obtained clemency from the colonial government for 11 of the 38 men who were convicted of murder in his court and unsuccessfully sought reprieves for some of the others who were eventually hanged.

The Travelling Judge

When Begbie was appointed the judge for British Columbia in 1858, the population of the new mainland colony consisted almost entirely of thousands of aliens (mostly Americans) who lived in remote mining camps along the Fraser River and, later, in the Interior. Most of these residents were unable, or refused, to travel to the colony's capital in New Westminster to settle their civil disputes or to be tried in criminal cases, so Begbie took British law to the camps. In January 1859, he sailed up the ice-filled Fraser River to Yale. The following month, Begbie walked from New Westminster to Lillooet and back, a distance of approximately 640 kilometres. Also in 1859, he walked from New Westminster to Kamloops and back (another 640 kilometres).

During the next 10 years, Begbie spent every fall and winter in New Westminster or along the lower Fraser River, and every spring and summer, he travelled to settlements on the upper Fraser and in the Cariboo. Eventually, as horses arrived and trails and roads were developed, the judge rode circuit across the entire colony; in 1865 alone, he travelled 5600 kilometres on horseback.

DID YOU  **KNOW?**

For many years, there were no courthouses in most of British Columbia's communities. If a barn or cabin was not available, Matthew Begbie held court while sitting on his horse or while seated behind a tree stump, always garbed in his judicial robes.

Blunt Speaking

Although Judge Matthew Begbie never told a jury what he thought of a defendant's guilt or innocence during a trial, he did occasionally give them a piece of his mind if they reached a verdict that he did not agree with. In 1862, in Williams Lake, a man named Gilchrist was found guilty of manslaughter instead of murder. While sentencing the defendant to life in prison, the imposing 195-centimetre-tall Begbie, with his thick moustache and beard, thundered: "Your crime was unmitigated, diabolical murder. You deserve to be hanged! Had the jury performed their duty, I might now have the painful satisfaction of condemning you to death." The judge then turned to the jury and told them that they were "a pack of Dallas horse-thieves, and permit me to say, it would give me great pleasure to see you hanged, each and every one of you, for declaring a murderer guilty only of manslaughter."

Identity Theft

In 1883, two Natives appeared before Judge Matthew Begbie on charges of robbery. As was common at the time, both of the accused used the names of prominent white men as nicknames, and one of them gave his name as "George Walkem" when he was arraigned. The real George Walkem was a former premier and fellow jurist, and he and Begbie had an intense dislike of each other. One can only imagine the smile on Begbie's face when he had a "George Walkem" appear before him as a defendant in a criminal case.

Enlightened for His Times

Unlike many in British Columbia in the mid and late 19th century, Judge Matthew Begbie was no bigot. Of the 11 convicted murderers that Begbie successfully sought clemency for between 1858 and 1871, nine were from the First Nations and two were Chinese. Begbie learned Shuswap and Chilcotin so well that he did not need an interpreter when those languages were spoken in court. He believed that the First Nations had aboriginal land rights and fought efforts to remove the Native peoples from their homes and land. And Begbie opposed bills in the British Columbia Legislative Assembly that were designed to discriminate against (and even expel) the Chinese in the province.

The Real Hanging Judges

Although Matthew Begbie is known as the "Hanging Judge," the title really belongs to two other men. A former Irish policeman, Peter O'Reilly held various judicial positions in British Columbia from 1859 until 1880. From 1859 to 1866, he was also the high sheriff of British Columbia. One of O'Reilly's duties was to arrange for the orderly hanging of condemned criminals.

O'Reilly's successor was Andrew Charles Elliott, a former judge in Yale and Lillooet. The position (but not the death penalty) was abolished in 1873, after which Elliott entered politics and later became premier.

The Cowboy Judge

The "Cowboy Judge"? That was Henry Castillou. He got the name from the cowboy boots and hat and the fringed buckskin jacket that he wore. Before becoming a county court judge in the Cariboo in 1950 (his courthouse was in Williams Lake), Castillou was one of the first attorneys to specialize in aboriginal rights, and he represented a number of BC's First Nations before the Indian Claims Commission.

Tall Justice

Judge W.R. "Willie" Williams of Phoenix, BC, weighed only 57 kilograms, but he was a towering 203 centimetres tall! Known for his love of wine, women and poker, Williams loved to boast that he was the "highest judge, in the highest court, in the highest city in Canada," and he was probably right. When Phoenix was incorporated as a city in 1900, its elevation was 1400 metres above sea level, making it the highest city in Canada. Nothing remains now of the old mining town except its cemetery.

TRANSCONTINENTAL RAILWAY

Protest Over Railroad Turns Violent

When British Columbia joined Confederation in 1871, it was with the understanding that the federal government build a transcontinental railway connecting BC with the rest of Canada. The railway was an important and sensitive issue to British Columbians; it would reduce the travel time between the province and the East from weeks and months to mere days. This in turn meant the arrival of more immigrants and goods to

BC and a connection to eastern Canada's markets. But in 1874, both British Columbia and the nation were in the grips of an economic depression. No railway tracks had yet been laid; indeed, the route for the railroad hadn't even been chosen. Dissatisfaction quickly spread, and demands that the Dominion live up to its agreement and "The terms, the whole terms and nothing but the terms!" became a battle cry.

Then, in early 1874, Premier Amor De Cosmos negotiated a deal with the feds whereby BC would get money for the building of a dry dock at Esquimalt in exchange for further delays in the railway's construction and an agreement that the anticipated Esquimalt–Nanaimo rail link would not be part of the transcontinental line. But when these terms were taken to the Legislative Assembly, all hell broke loose! Hundreds of angry protestors stormed the Birdcages (as the province's legislative buildings were commonly known) on February 7. James Trimble, the Speaker of the Assembly, was literally forced from his chair, and the premier had to hide in the Speaker's chamber for his own safety. Two days later, De Cosmos resigned.

Let's Break Up the Country!

Anger in BC over the federal government's failure to build the transcontinental railway finally reached a boiling point when, on August 29, 1878, the Legislative Assembly voted 15 to 9 in favour of a resolution sponsored by Premier George Walkem asking Queen Victoria "to see fit to order and direct that British Columbia shall have the right…to withdraw from the Union" with Canada. That got Ottawa's attention! Construction on the railway began soon afterwards and was completed in 1885.

FAITH IN GOD

The Bachelor Polygamist

British Columbia's first convert to Mormonism was Anthony Maitland Stenhouse. The Comox farmer and politician even resigned his seat in the BC legislature in 1887 so he could serve the church. Although he initially planned to go to Utah, he ended up at the Mormon community in Lethbridge, North West Territories (now Alberta), and quickly became known across Canada for his defence of polygamy. Among other things, Stenhouse claimed that the practice advanced the cause of women's rights! The former British Columbian brought enough attention to the matter that the Canadian Parliament passed a law in 1890 to strengthen the ban against bigamy. The Mormon Church later decided that same year not to solemnize any more plural marriages and, with that, Stenhouse's cause was dead. Ironically, Stenhouse was a lifelong bachelor.

The Stolen Church

Ever steal a church? St. Peter's Anglican Church was built in 1887 in Donald, where the Canadian Pacific Railway located its divisional point. Ten years later, the CPR transferred the divisional point to nearby Revelstoke, and most of the towns-folk (and buildings!) followed. However, two of Donald's residents, Mr. and Mrs. Kimpton, preferred Windermere instead. It did not take long for Mrs. Kimpton to miss her old church, so she had her husband steal it (nails and all) and ship it, by wagon and barge, to Windermere (a distance of over 200 kilometres), where it was rebuilt over the objections of the Kimpton's former neighbours. And the church has been there ever since.

The Oldest Church

Despite Yale's well-deserved reputation for being a den of inequity during the Fraser River Gold Rush (1858–61), it did have a place of refuge for the righteous. The oldest church in British Columbia that is still on its original foundation and still in use (though now as a heritage building) is the town's St. John the Divine Church, which was built in 1859.

EFFECTS OF WESTERN CONTACT

Collapse of a Civilization

Estimates of the First Nations pre-contact (pre-1774) population in BC vary from 75,000 to 400,000. Whatever it was originally, it had fallen to below 26,000 by 1871. The decrease could be primarily attributed to various diseases brought to British Columbia by the European traders, miners and settlers.

The Nuu-chah-nulth

One example of the dramatic decline in BC's First Nations' population after their first contact with Europeans is the Nuu-chah-nulth on the west coast of Vancouver Island. There were about 28,000 of them in the late 18th century, but they numbered less than 2000 when the 1931 census was taken. There are now about 6000 Nuu-chah-nulth in the province.

DID YOU  KNOW?

Two BC First Nations bands have disappeared entirely since Europeans came to British Columbia: the Pentlatch, who lived on the eastern shore of Vancouver Island, and the Tsetsaut, who resided in the north-central Interior near Meziadin Lake.

The Biggest Killer: Smallpox!

Of all the diseases brought to British Columbia by Europeans, smallpox was the greatest killer. The first epidemic occurred in 1782, and there was another in 1836–38. The third outbreak of the disease occurred in 1862–63.

In March 1862, an infected sailor from San Francisco stepped off his ship while in Victoria. The disease quickly spread to First Nations settlements on the outskirts of town, where large numbers of Natives lived every summer while working as labourers for the local colonists before returning to their villages for the winter. By May, the authorities, at the urging of Victoria's residents, who were afraid of smallpox, began to evict the aboriginals and burn down their homes. With nowhere to go, the Natives returned to their villages along the coast and the Interior and, unintentionally, spread the disease everywhere they went. By the end of 1863, over 19,000 First Nations people (or over 40 percent of the First Nations population in BC) had died of smallpox.

First Nations' Loss While BC's Numbers Grow

When British Columbia became a province in 1871, approximately 71 percent of its population (just under 26,000 of BC's 36,000 residents) was aboriginal. Indeed, until the 1880s, most of BC's inhabitants were First Nations. But as waves of immigrants flooded into the province, the First Nations population actually decreased to about 20,000, primarily because of high infant mortality rates. Then, beginning in the 1920s, the province's Native population hovered at around 25,000 for about 20 years. Since that time, BC's First Nations population has steadily grown.

LANGUAGES

The Jargon

A hybrid language consisting of words from Chehalis, Chinook, Nuu-chah-nulth, English and French was used along the west coast of North America from Alaska to California, including British Columbia, to facilitate commerce among the many First Nations bands and between the First Nations and European traders and settlers. Commonly referred to today as "Chinook Jargon," it actually had a number of names along the West Coast and was also simply known in many areas as "the Chinook," "the Jargon" or as "the old trade language." With a limited vocabulary of only about 700 words, Chinook Jargon actually pre-dates the Europeans' first contact with the First Nations of BC, and it incorporated English and French words after Europeans began to trade with the local aboriginal populations.

In the 1880s, a writing system was created for Chinook Jargon, and from 1891 until 1923, there was a newspaper printed in British Columbia, the *Kamloops Wawa*, that was written in the language. Chinook Jargon also came to be used in missionary work, newspaper advertising and court testimony.

During its height in the 19th century, about 250,000 people spoke Chinook Jargon in BC and the western United States, but it fell into disuse when English became the dominant language of the First Nations people. Today, only a few people can still speak Jargon, but several words (for example, "potlatch," "high muckamucks" and "cultus," as in Cultus Lake) are in common usage.

Boston Men

Because the first Americans who came to British Columbia were fur traders from Boston, Massachusetts, for years the First Nations people in BC referred to all Americans as "Boston Men." The British who came to British Columbia, however, were known as "King George's Men." And, yes, the First Nations people knew the difference.

Lost Languages

Not counting dialects and minor variations, 32 of Canada's 60 distinct First Nations languages are native to British Columbia. However, three of them—Nicola, Pentlatch and Tsetsaut—are extinct, with no living speakers, and there are several languages that are spoken by less than 100 people.

COASTAL FIRST NATIONS EMPIRE AND CLASH WITH AMERICANS

Emperor of Vancouver Island

Chief Wickaninnish of the Tla-o-qui-aht First Nation of Clayoquot Sound (one of the Nuu-chah-nulth peoples) was the most powerful man on Vancouver Island in the late 18th and early 19th centuries, when European and American seafarers started to trade with BC's local inhabitants. His name meant "no one in front of him in the canoe," and he controlled a vast territory along the western coast of Vancouver Island and northern Washington State. Up to 13,000 people lived within Wickaninnish's realm. At Clayoquot Sound alone, there were at least five villages of 1500 residents each (including one with over 2500 people). This has led some to refer to Wickaninnish as the "Emperor of Vancouver Island."

Past Sins Forgiven

During the winter of 1791–92, American sea captain Robert Gray and his men wintered on Meares Island at a post they called Fort Defiance. That spring, six violent encounters between Gray's crew and the local Nuu-chah-nulth First Nations people (the Tla-o-qui-aht) led Gray to mistakenly believe that the Natives were plotting against him, so the captain kidnapped the son of their chief, Wickaninnish, to use as a hostage. That led to an attack on Gray's encampment. In retaliation, Gray had the 200 homes and other buildings at the Tla-o-qui-aht village of Opitsat on Meares Island burned to the ground before he sailed away. The charred remains of the village were found nearly 200 years later in the 1980s. The discovery caused Gray's descendant, William Twombly, to reflect upon what his ancestor had done. In 2005, with 13 of his cousins, Twombly sailed to

Meares Island on a replica of Gray's *Lady Washington* and, following the protocol recommended by the Tla-o-qui-aht band leaders, read an apology to the local inhabitants from the rails of the ship. Twombly's statement was warmly received, and a big party was held with him as the guest of honour.

An Explosive Encounter

In 1811, the nearly 30-metre-long American trading vessel, the *Tonquin*, arrived at Clayoquot Sound near present-day Tofino. The ship was owned by New York millionaire John Jacob Astor and was part of Astor's plan to break the British and Russian monopoly of the Pacific fur trade. While negotiating for furs with the Tla-o-qui-aht First Nation, the ship's captain, Jonathan Thorn, slapped the band's chief, Wickaninnish, with a sea otter pelt. This may have brought back memories to Wickaninnish of 20 years before, when another American sea captain, Robert Gray, had kidnapped his son and burned down his village. Whatever the reason, scores of Tla-o-qui-aht warriors attacked the *Tonquin* the next day and killed all but one of its 23-member crew before the ship's wounded clerk set the 4 tonnes of gunpowder in the *Tonquin's* magazine on fire. The ship disappeared in one massive explosion, and the bay was covered with debris, bodies and Natives crying for help or swimming for their lives. Over 150 Tla-o-qui-aht (some say as many as 200) were killed. Needless to say, the whole incident had a significant impact on the relations between the European and American traders and the local First Nations. Western seafarers avoided Clayoquot Sound and most of the west coast of Vancouver Island for the next 50 years.

DID YOU KNOW?

The destruction of the *Tonquin* and the events that led up to it were dramatized in the 1941 movie *This Woman is Mine* (later re-released as *Fury at Sea*, starring three-time Academy–winner Walter Brennan. This picture was nominated for an Oscar for Best Musical Score.

Who Was Taking Advantage of Whom?

Who benefited the most in the late 18th and early 19th centuries from the sea otter trade between the American and European seafarers and the First Nations peoples of BC depended entirely upon one's point of view. For example, American sea captain John Kendrick once received sea otter pelts that he could sell for $8000 in exchange for about $100 worth of various small items, and such exchanges were the rule, not the exception. No wonder the Russians referred to the sea otter pelts as "soft gold." But according to the First Nations people at the time, they were the ones who reaped great benefits from the trade. In exchange for the "few trifling furs" that they gave to the Americans and Europeans, the Natives got items that were of immeasurable value to them, such as axes, chisels, cloth and iron.

SPANISH COLUMBIA?

The First Spanish Visit

Notwithstanding rumours that Sir Francis Drake may have reached the BC coast in 1579, it was the Spanish who were the first Europeans to visit British Columbia. Worried about Russian territorial ambitions, the Spanish sent naval captain Juan Perez and his ship, the *Santiago*, from Baja California to take possession of the Northwest Coast in 1774. Perez sailed as far as the northern tip of the Queen Charlotte Islands and traded with the local Haida First Nation. On his way back south, Perez stopped at the mouth of Nootka Sound and traded there with the Nuu-chah-nulth. On both occasions, Perez and his men stayed on their ships because they feared an attack by the First Nations, and it was the Natives who came to them. But by not going ashore, Perez was not able to claim the island for Spain.

The Spanish at Nootka Sound

The first permanent European settlement in British Columbia was Spanish. It was established at present-day Yuquot in Nootka Sound in 1789, and a fort was built there (the first permanent European military presence in BC) a year later. The settlers and troops left British Columbia in 1795 and haven't been back since, but they did leave behind a number of Spanish place names, including Alberni, Quadra and Juan de Fuca.

Did the Spanish Arrive in the BC Interior?
While the 1774 voyage of Captain Juan Perez to the Queen Charlottes and Nootka Sound is the first recorded Spanish visit to British Columbia, there may have been an earlier one.

According to the oral history of the Similkameen First Nation, an expedition of strange-looking men with white faces and metal clothes came from the south sometime in the mid 18th century. Pictographs in the area also depict horses and headgear that strongly resemble, Spanish helmets. The strangers camped near present-day Keremeos until a disagreement between one of them and a First Nations person turned into a small war. After many Similkameen were killed, the white-faced men went north with prisoners and wintered near present-day Kelowna. They came back in the spring and set up camp on a flat overlooking the Keremeos River. This time, the Similkameen wiped them out. After the battle, the remains, weapons and armour of the strangers were buried at a spot (the exact location of which is unknown) now called Spanish Mound.

COLONIAL BRITISH COLUMBIA'S IDENTITY CRISIS!

Just How Many Colonies Were There?

The first British colony established on the Pacific Coast of North America was Vancouver Island in 1849. The next was the Queen Charlotte Islands, which became a colony in 1852. Most of the BC mainland became the colony of British Columbia in 1858. The Stikine Territory, the northern third of present-day BC, was split from the North-Western Territory (a region that included the present-day Yukon, Northwest Territories, eastern Nunavut and northern Alberta and Saskatchewan) and became a separate colony in 1862. The next year, both the Queen Charlotte Islands and Stikine colonies were merged into British Columbia. And, in 1866, Vancouver Island and British Columbia were united into one large colony. Got that?

What's My Job Title Again?

For a while, Sir James Douglas was the colonial governor of Vancouver Island, the Queen Charlottes, the Stikine Territory and British Columbia all at the same time!

DID YOU KNOW?

Ever hear of New Caledonia? Or Albertoria? Borelia? Nigrentia? Pacifica? West Britannia? No? These were all names considered in 1858 for Britain's newest colony on the west coast of North America (the present-day BC mainland) before Queen Victoria settled on "British Columbia."

What Happened to New Caledonia?

The explorer Simon Fraser named the BC Interior between the Rocky and the Coast Mountains "New Caledonia," which means "New Scotland," because of its resemblance to the Scottish Highlands as described by his mother. New Caledonia was also going to be the moniker of the new mainland colony established in 1858, but the name was changed to Queen Victoria's choice, "British Columbia," at the last moment. The reason for the switch was that France already had a colony called New Caledonia in the Pacific. And when the British colonies on Vancouver Island and the mainland were combined in 1866, the name "British Columbia" was applied to the new entity as well.

ALAS, POOR GOVERNOR KENNEDY

Experienced Governor!

Arthur Edward Kennedy, the third and last governor of Vancouver Island, was a man whose work took him all over the world. Before he was sent to Victoria in 1864, he had been the British colonial governor of Sierra Leone in Africa and of Western Australia. After leaving British Columbia two years later (when Vancouver Island and the mainland BC colony were merged and his job disappeared), he went on to become the governor of West Africa, Hong Kong and the Queensland colony in Australia.

The Governor's Low Opinion of His Constituents

While Arthur Kennedy was governor of Vancouver Island from 1864 to 1866, he had few positive things to say about the colony's residents. According to Kennedy, there were two kinds of people residing there: "those who are convicts and those who ought to be convicts."

Mutual Dislike

Governor Kennedy's intense dislike for the residents of Vancouver Island was reciprocated. The colonists didn't care much for his attempt to curtail the illegal sale of whiskey to First Nations peoples. They also did not like his idea of recognizing aboriginal land claims nor of allowing Natives to testify in court. Kennedy's belief that Vancouver Island's union with the mainland colony of British Columbia should be under terms favourable to both colonies and not just to the island didn't sit too well either. Kennedy was called "deranged," and the colonial legislature initially denied him money to pay for an office, clerical assistance and even office supplies. They also denied him an official residence, and Kennedy and his family had to live in a hotel! When Kennedy finally left Vancouver Island in 1866, the general feeling was one of "goodbye and good riddance."

POPULATION ODDITIES

Who's in Charge Here?

In 1870, the year before it entered Confederation, British Columbia's population consisted of 8576 people of European descent, 462 blacks and 1548 Chinese. The aboriginal population was just under 26,000. However, the First Nations people had no say in how the colony was run.

Where Can a Guy Get a Date?

Not counting the First Nations population, in 1870, British Columbia was a predominately male society where men outnumbered women by more than two to one. On the mainland, the ratio was even more lopsided. In Lillooet, among the non-Native population, there were 35 women to the town's 203 men (and 80 Chinese men). The combined populations of Hope, Lytton and Yale included 660 men but only 96 women (and 311 Chinese men). In Kootenay, there were only five women to the region's 105 men (and 139 Chinese males). Only in Victoria, which had a population of 3561, and the surrounding communities were the male and female populations approximately equal. And the male–female ratio was even worse among the colony's Chinese population. Of the over 1500 Chinese in BC in 1870, a mere 53 of them were women!

The Love Boat

On September 18, 1862, a news correspondent for the *Victoria Colonist* reported on the special cargo that arrived in Esquimalt aboard the *Tynemouth* from England. "Cleanly, well built, pretty looking... We are highly pleased with the appearance of the 'invoice.'" But the reporter wasn't writing about anything you'd find at the local Hudson's Bay Company store. Instead, he was describing the 60 women (plus one strict matron), some as young as 14 and virtually all in their teens, who had been sponsored by the Columbia Emigration Society (an agency of the Anglican Church) to sail around the world for 99 days, hoping to find a better future in the New World than they faced back in Britain. The ship was welcomed by hundreds of noisy and celebrating men who couldn't wait to get a good look at the female passengers. One young lady, the moment she stepped on shore, was offered a proposal of marriage that was immediately accepted, to the cheers of the crowd; the two were married the very next day. Indeed, within six months, half of the girls were either married or had jobs as governesses and servants. Another "brideship," the *Robert Lowe*, arrived with 36 women three months later.

Emma

Emma Helen Tammadge had perhaps the most successful future of all the ladies who arrived in Esquimalt aboard the brideship *Tynemouth* in 1862. In 1867, she married an Overlander (an Ontarian who crossed the width of Canada in 1862 in search of BC gold) named Richard Henry Alexander. Alexander later became a prominent businessman and local politician in Vancouver. Together, the couple would become an integral part of BC's political and social elite.

But Emma was a remarkable woman in her own right. The first woman of European descent to live in present-day Vancouver, she was a friend, advisor and doctor (though she had no formal training) to the First Nations peoples around Burrard Inlet. Tammadge was also in charge of the relief money collected after the 1886 fire that destroyed Vancouver and was one of the founders of the Victorian Order of Nurses.

CAN YOU KEEP A SECRET?

Finding the Gold

The Haida first discovered gold in the Queen Charlotte Islands in 1851. That led to prospecting on other coastal islands and in the lower mainland of New Caledonia (present-day British Columbia). The Hudson's Bay Company supplied the aboriginals with equipment to keep them digging and panning, and indeed, the First Nations found more gold along the Fraser River in 1853 and near the Thompson River on the mainland three years later. However, James Douglas, the HBC's chief factor at Fort Victoria and the colonial governor of Vancouver Island (and, as such, the British authority closest in proximity to the gold sites), feared an invasion of American prospectors into the unsettled mainland if word of the discoveries got out, so he tried to keep everything quiet. Douglas' attempts at secrecy worked until 1858. That February, the HBC shipped nearly 1000 ounces of Fraser River gold to the mint in San Francisco. The mint's superintendent was a member of the local volunteer fire department and, unfortunately, a blabbermouth. One day, while on drill, he let slip to his fellow firefighters the news about the gold shipment.

On March 12, 1858, the first 15 gold prospectors from San Francisco sailed for Victoria. Within a week, they were at the mouth of the Fraser River near present-day Yale, and on March 20, discovered at Hill's Bar (near Yale) the largest single deposit of gold (over $2 million in 1858 dollars) ever found during the Fraser River Gold Rush. Word quickly spread across the entire world, and Douglas' secret was out.

Where Are the Hotels?

On April 25, 1858, the *Commodore* arrived in Victoria from San Francisco with 450 prospectors on their way to the Fraser River goldfields. Doubling the town's population, the miners had to sleep in tents because Victoria did not yet have any hotels.

Talk About Inflation!

Over 20,000 gold miners arrived in Victoria in 1858. The vast majority went on to the goldfields along the Fraser River, but some stayed, and the sudden influx of people, both transient and permanent, resulted in wild increases in the price of real estate. City lots in Victoria that once sold for only $25 apiece were, one week later, going for $3000 each!

WHO WERE THESE MEN?

Gold Seekers Were a Mixed Bag

In the last two weeks of May 1858 alone, at least 10,000 Californians passed through Victoria on their way to the Fraser River goldfields. By the end of the year, up to 30,000 prospectors (most of them arriving through Victoria) were searching for gold along the Fraser between Hope and Lillooet, with some as far north as Quesnel. But while most of the prospectors were from the United States, only a third were Americans. The rest included British and French as well as Belgians, Chileans, Chinese, Danes, Germans, Hawaiians, Hungarians, Italians, Mexicans, Poles, Spaniards, Swedes, West Indians and even colonists from Lower Canada (Ontario), Upper Canada (Québec) and the Maritimes (such as the famous Amor De Cosmos), all of whom had gone to California during the preceding decade to strike it rich in that state's gold rush.

DID YOU KNOW?

California wasn't the only place where gold miners came from during the Fraser River Gold Rush. Some came from the depleted goldfields of Australia, too!

Not All Were Miners
Of the 30,000 individuals who arrived during the Fraser River Gold Rush, only a quarter of them actually searched for gold. The others included gamblers, claim jumpers, prostitutes, land speculators and businessmen of every kind, all intent on making a living by providing whatever services the miners needed or by stealing the miners' gold.

How Do We Get There?

Between 25,000 and 35,000 prospectors stampeded into British Columbia during the Fraser River and Cariboo Gold Rushes. Most sailed from San Francisco to Victoria (the only legal point of entry into BC), crossed over to the mainland and then travelled by boat, horse or foot up the Fraser River to their destination. However, approximately 8000 skipped Victoria and went through Oregon and Washington to get to the goldfields; some also travelled across the continent from eastern Canada.

YALE

Where's the Gold?

The richest discoveries of fine gold during the Fraser River Gold Rush were in the 13 kilometres between Hope and Yale.

Tremendous Population Growth

Located at the mouth of the Fraser Canyon, there was nothing at Yale in March 1858 but a single "fort" (without stockade) made from logs and used as a stopover by the Hudson's Bay Company's annual brigades into the Interior. But the discovery of gold at nearby Hill's Bar on March 23 changed all that. Within weeks, between 700 and 800 men were living there, most of them in canvas tents. And because Yale marked the beginning of the Cariboo Wagon Road, as well as the point where steamboats could no longer travel up the Fraser River, Yale became a prosperous inland port. By the end of 1858, it boasted a population of 1800 permanent and temporary residents, making it the largest community at the time on the mainland of present-day British Columbia. And it continued to grow! During the next two years, its population would fluctuate between 5000 and 8000.

The Best and the Worst

Yale was the "busiest and worst town in the colony" during the Fraser River Gold Rush. Every other store was a saloon and gambling house. There were 13 drinking establishments on Front Street alone. Criminals of every kind, as well as pugilists, prostitutes and soldiers from the U.S. army who had deserted to join the gold rush, all wandered freely on its streets with virtually no interference from the law. Indeed, the law consisted of only the gold commissioner (a judicial officer) and two constables. Assaults and robberies, as well as the occasional murder, were common occurrences; one man was even killed because he refused to pay for his drink of whiskey!

War Zone

During the height of the Fraser River Gold Rush, Yale's population was normally between 5000 and 8000. However, it jumped overnight to 15,000 for a short time in 1858 because of the evacuations caused by the brief Fraser Canyon War between the local miners and the Nlaka'pamux First Nation, who lived in the canyon.

Exodus

The Fraser River Gold Rush was short-lived. Although it began in 1858, only two years later, the gold along the Fraser was depleted, and most of the miners had returned to the United States or drifted farther into the BC Interior in search of the elusive metal. By 1861, most of the miners that were left along the Fraser River were Chinese who were not allowed to prospect anywhere except at abandoned sites and who made only a few dollars a day for their efforts.

GOLD IN THE CARIBOO!

Who Were the Argonauts?

In the early 1860s, if you mentioned the Argonauts, you weren't referring to the companions of the Greek mythological character Jason who joined him in search of the Golden Fleece. (And you certainly would not have been referring to the Toronto Argonauts football team, which was not created until 1873.) Instead, you would have been talking about the men from eastern Canada who flocked to the Cariboo in search of gold.

DID YOU KNOW?

Unlike the Fraser River Gold Rush, during which the largest group of prospectors were Americans, most of the miners involved in the Cariboo Gold Rush, which started when the ore was discovered at Horsefly in 1859, were British and Canadian.

"Hanging Judge" O'Reilly

Wild Horse Creek, now a ghost town near Fort Steele, was a community of 5000 to 6000 souls during the Cariboo Gold Rush. The original settlement was called Fisherville, but had to be relocated and all of its buildings torn down when it was discovered that the town sat on top of a rich gold deposit. Wild Horse Creek was also a lawless place with shootings and killings. So when Judge Peter O'Reilly arrived, he gathered all the residents together and told them: "Now, boys, there must be no shooting, for if there is a shooting there will surely be a hanging!" The judge knew of what he spoke since he was also the High Sheriff of British Columbia, and thus personally responsible for carrying out the lawful executions in the colony. O'Reilly's threat did the trick; the violent crime rate in Wild Horse Creek immediately dropped to zero.

Camels in BC!

Frank Laumeister had a wonderful idea. In 1862, the Lillooet
entrepreneur imported 21 camels from California to use as pack
animals to carry supplies up the Cariboo Road to the goldfields.
He paid $300 each for 23 camels, but two did not arrive. The
animals could each carry about 180 kilograms—more than any
horse or mule—but they proved more trouble than they were
worth, and Laumeister let them go after a year. The camels' feet
were used to sand and were easily damaged when they walked
on the rough and rocky Cariboo Road. They didn't smell too
good either; their odour was so bad that it literally caused horses,
mules and oxen to stampede. The camels were also hard to
handle, spat on people when upset and ate clothes and soap.
Within four months, the BC legislature outlawed the use of

camels on the Cariboo Road. In the end, Laumeister sold some of the camels, killed some for their meat and just let the others loose to roam free and fend for themselves in the wilderness. The last of the 21 camels died near Ashcroft in 1905 (some sources say 1910), but some people claimed to have seen their offspring living wild in the Thompson Country and the Camelsfoot Range near Lillooet until the 1950s.

Ever Hear of the Overlanders?

The Overlanders were the approximately 150 Ontarians who met in 1862 at Fort Garry, near present-day Winnipeg, and set out that June for the Cariboo goldfields. They were mostly young bachelors but were accompanied by a very pregnant, 27-year-old Catherine Schubert, her husband, Augustus, and their three small children. The Overlanders crossed the Prairies and the Rocky Mountains by cart and packhorse until they reached Tête Jaune Cache some 266 kilometres east of Prince George. (By taking this trip, Catherine became the first woman known to cross Canada.) From Tête Jaune Cache, the Schuberts and some of the Overlanders travelled down the Thompson River by canoe and raft. None of the Overlanders became rich in the goldfields, but many later achieved great success in other careers. On October 14, 1862, shortly after arriving in present-day Kamloops, Mrs. Schubert gave birth to a girl. The baby, named Rose, was the first child of European descent born in the BC Interior.

"Twelve Foot" Davis

Henry Fuller Davis was an American who came to BC during the Cariboo Gold Rush. Between two claims that were producing a lot of gold for their owners, Davis discovered a small, 3.7-metre-wide (that's 12 feet in imperial measurements) strip of unclaimed land. Davis quickly filed his own claim and, in a short time, extracted $12,000 (some sources say $15,000) worth of gold out of it! For the rest of his life, he was called "Twelve Foot" Davis—he's even identified by that name on his tombstone.

Dr. Davis?

After striking it rich during the Cariboo Gold Rush, Henry "Twelve Foot" Davis went to the Peace River area and used his wealth to establish several trading posts. He also maintained an outfit of packhorses.

Davis signed registers with the initials "MD" following his name whenever he stayed at a hotel. It wasn't because he was a physician, but as he explained: "After all, I am a genuine mule driver."

"Cariboo" Cameron

John A. Cameron, a Cariboo prospector, was devoted to his wife, Margaret Sophia Cameron. The couple was originally from Glengarry County, Upper Canada (now Ontario), and when Margaret died of typhoid fever in 1862, he kept his promise to send her body there for burial. Cameron and one of his partners took Mrs. Cameron's remains 640 kilometres by toboggan from Williams Creek to Victoria, a trip that took five weeks. Then, after placing the body in an alcohol-filled coffin, Cameron buried his wife in Victoria and temporarily returned to the Cariboo to work his claim, which had hit the "motherlode" shortly after Margaret's death. In October 1863, Cameron left the Cariboo and, taking the coffin with him, returned as a rich man to Glengarry County. But over time, rumours began to circulate that Margaret wasn't dead, but had been sold off to a First Nations chief, and that the buried coffin was full of gold! After 10 years of innuendo and lies, "Cariboo" Cameron had the coffin dug up and opened. When it was, everyone saw the face of Margaret Cameron—almost perfectly preserved in the alcohol.

Whiskey as Hair Tonic!

Ever hear of Jean Jacques Caux? No? Well, how about Cataline the Packer, the most famous pack-train driver in British Columbia? He began his business in Yale and Ashcroft in 1858 during the Fraser River Gold Rush and continued until his retirement in 1913 at the age of 83! During those 55 years, the native of Catalonia (in the French Pyrenees) would use mules to transport goods all across the BC mainland and even into Alaska and the Yukon.

Known as the most honest and reliable packer in the Cariboo, only once did Caux lose a load. This happened when one of his employees tossed away a strange-smelling package that he thought contained something rotten—it was an order of Limburger cheese. Caux was also a little eccentric. He would rub whiskey (some sources say cognac) into his long, curly, black hair ("A lidda insida, a lidda outsida. *Bon!* She maka da hair grow!"). Caux was also known for taking baths every day in icy cold streams and rolling around naked in the snow every morning in the winter. In addition, though he spoke little English (whenever anyone asked his name, he would merely reply "Catalonia"—hence, his nickname), Caux could swear in seven languages. And he was an expert at throwing knives.

Barker's Bonanza

Most of the 25,000 to 30,000 prospectors who came to British Columbia during the Fraser River and Cariboo Gold Rushes did not strike it rich. Even if they did, there was no guarantee that they'd hold on to their money. Take William Barker. He became tremendously wealthy when he found gold along Williams Creek in northern BC in 1862. His claim yielded $600,000 in the shiny metal by 1866, which would be worth millions today. Barkerville, which is located near his find, is named after him. But Barker quickly spent his fortune, and he ended his days as a pauper in the Old Men's Home in Victoria.

ODDS AND ENDS

Have Left Lillooet for Barkerville!

For a short while during the Fraser River Gold Rush days, Lillooet had an estimated population of 16,000 (!!!) and was known as the "largest town north of San Francisco and west of Chicago" (which was true). But once the gold ran out, so did the miners; the town's population in 1870 was a mere 318. (Even today, Lillooet is less than one-eighth its former size.)

Lillooet's loss was Barkerville's gain. Shortly after gold was discovered along Williams Creek in 1862, Barkerville was established, and it soon became the second largest city in North America west of the Mississippi (San Francisco was still first) with a population of 5000.

Build Me a Road That Lasts

An overland road between New Westminster and Yale was finally built in the 1870s. Until then, the only way to travel between these two locations was by boat. The route went through Surrey, Abbotsford and Chilliwack and parts of it, known as the Old Yale Road, are still in use today.

MINING

Silver Mountain

Chikamin is Chinook Jargon for "metal" or "ore." Often, the word is used to mean "money." And Chikamin Mountain on the eastern side of Kootenay Lake is well named. During the last part of the 19th century, fur traders and Natives would travel there whenever they ran out of musket balls; the metal from the mountain was so rich that it could be shaped into little round balls without being melted and poured into moulds. And the reason the ore was so malleable was that it contained high amounts of lead and silver! Later, Chikamin Mountain was the site of one of the richest lead and silver mines in Canada, the Blue Bell Mine.

The Big Boulder

In 1892, amateur prospector J.W. Cockle was cutting a pole while standing on top of a boulder near Sandon, BC. Cockle's axe slipped and cut away a chunk of the rock. The miner instantly recognized the exposed ore as galena. What Cockle had discovered was the largest silver nugget ever found! It was 2.25 metres long, nearly one metre wide, 2.75 metres high and weighed between 109 and 113 tonnes. Cockle and his partner staked a claim for the spot where the nugget sat and sold the rock, later known as the "Big Boulder," for $2000 to a man who wanted to exhibit it at the 1893 Chicago World's Fair.

However, the rock never got there. Instead, it was broken up, melted down and over $20,000 (almost $400,000 in today's dollars) in silver was taken out of it. And the land where the nugget was found? Worthless! More experienced miners quickly determined that the boulder had rolled down a nearby mountainside hundreds of years earlier, and that its original location was already the site of someone else's silver mine. But the photograph of Cockle and his partner standing next to the Big Boulder was printed in newspapers around the world and led to a stampede of miners into the mountains surrounding Slocan Lake.

You See, I Shot This Deer and…

In 1888, Dr. Alex A. Forbes, a part-time prospector, came across some interesting rock samples in Vancouver and went up Howe Sound to investigate their origin. While there, Forbes shot at a buck at Britannia Mountain, and the fleeing deer's hooves exposed some metal underneath the moss. It was copper! It took a while for anything to happen as a result of the discovery, but mining began in 1904, and a town quickly grew up around the site. By 1929, the Britannia Beach copper mines were the largest in the Commonwealth.

LOVE, HATE AND A SMALL CITY

I Still Can't Get a Date!

In 1871, the year that British Columbia joined Confederation, men outnumbered women by almost three to one. That ratio did not change very rapidly. As late as 1911, over 70 percent of British Columbia's population was still male. In 1921, nearly 60 percent of BC's residents were men, and the figures weren't much better 10 years later. It was not until the 1950s that the genders became approximately equal in number in the province. And since 1981, the ladies have been in the majority.

The Lusitania Riots

Anti-German feeling in British Columbia during World War I reached its peak when a German submarine sank the British passenger ship, the *Lusitania*, on May 7, 1915. Among the nearly 1200 passengers and crew who lost their lives were 15 residents of Victoria, including James Dunsmuir Jr., the son of the financier and former premier. Rumours quickly spread that the local German population in Victoria was celebrating the sinking and that German submarines would soon cut off Vancouver Island from the rest of the province. In response, angry mobs, fuelled by alcohol and patriotic bravado, gathered in downtown Victoria on the night of May 8 and demolished several businesses that were owned by German Canadians or had German-sounding names. They even tried to storm Government House, where Lieutenant-Governor Francis Bernard lived, because Bernard's wife was from a prominent German Canadian family. The greatly outnumbered Victoria police did nothing to stop the rioting, and troops were required to restore order. The next night, the mob struck again, this time attacking Chinese as well as German establishments. Almost immediately, local businesses began to advertise that they had no German connections or employees, several German Canadians lost their jobs because their employers feared the loss of business or damage to their property from the rioters, and a number of German-born residents of the city left their homes (many for good) for refuge in the United States.

Canada's Smallest City

With a population of only 666 (2003 estimate), Greenwood, BC, is Canada's smallest city. But this wasn't always the case. Founded in 1895 and incorporated as a "city" two years later, the mining town once boasted 3000 residents, but the collapse of the local mining industry after World War I almost destroyed the community. Greenwood got a new lease on life during World War II, when it was picked as the site of one of the camps where Japanese Canadians were interned. After the war, many of the internees decided to stay in Greenwood. And through all the years, the community has never given up its designation as a "city."

The Kingdom of Vancouver Island?

In September 1882, Canada's new governor general, the Marquis of Lorne, came to Victoria for a two-week visit. Accompanying him was his wife, Princess Louise, who was one of Queen Victoria's daughters. The couple proved to be tremendously popular, and the visit became a three-month stay. And while Lord Lorne was off touring various parts of the province, the princess stayed in the city named after her mother and continued to wow the local crowd. In fact, she was so popular that when the vice-regal visit neared its end, Premier Robert Beaven suggested that Louise be proclaimed queen of an independent Vancouver Island!

LITERACY COMES TO BRITISH COLUMBIA

Nonfiction

The first book (aside from government publications) written and printed in British Columbia was Alfred Waddington's 1858 work, *The Fraser Mines Vindicated; or A History of Four Months*. It was intended to stem the exodus of British colonists from Vancouver Island to the goldfields on the mainland. The book's success is debatable.

Romance

The first novel whose story was set in British Columbia was Morley Roberts' 1892 masterpiece *The Mate of the Vancouver*. It was a romance about a man who comes to BC in pursuit of a girl while a nasty villain is after him. *The Mate of the Vancouver*, however, was not the first novel published in British Columbia; it was printed instead in London, England. (The first novel published in BC was 1895's *As It Was In The Fifties* by the editor of the *Province*, Arthur Hodgins Scaife, who wrote under the pseudonym Kim Bilir.) *The Mate of the Vancouver* was also not Roberts' first book about British Columbia; that was *The Western Avernus* (1887), which was a factual account of Roberts' first three years in BC. Roberts later wrote more than two dozen other novels, as well as memories, biographies, books about cancer research and international politics and hundreds of short stories. He also wrote an autobiography, but the manuscript was lost in the mail and never found.

DID YOU KNOW?

It was *The Western Avernus* that led a young Scottish banker named Robert Service to immigrate to Canada.

Emily Carr, Writer?

The Governor General's Literary Awards were established in 1937 to honour Canada's greatest writers in fiction, nonfiction, poetry and other categories. The first two British Columbians to receive the prize took home the award in 1941. One was Joyce Anne Marriott, who won for her second book of poetry, *Calling Adventurers*. Marriott afterwards continued writing poetry as well as working as a scriptwriter for the CBC and the National Film Board and as a newspaper journalist in Prince George.

The other BC writer to win the GG's Award that year was painter Emily Carr for her collection of short, nonfiction pieces entitled *Klee Wyck*. Carr used the First Nations culture of British Columbia and southern Alaska coastline as the focus of her art-work, but success did not come before she went broke and had to give it all up in 1913. She was then employed as a boarding-house keeper, potter, dog breeder and raiser of hens and rabbits for the next 15 years. But Carr met fellow artist Lauren Harris in 1927, and he encouraged her to get back into painting. By the 1930s, she was recognized as one of Canada's greatest painters. (One of her paintings sold for over $1 million in 2004.) Carr started writing in 1941 at the age of 70, while she was in hospi-tal recuperating from a heart attack. She gave her work the nick-name that was given to her by the Nuu-chah-nulth First Nation when she visited their reserve on Vancouver Island in 1898. ("Klee Wyck" means "laughing one.") And it was that book, her first, that won Carr the Governor General's prize.

DID YOU KNOW?

British Columbia has its own version of the Governor General's Literary Awards. The BC Book Prizes were established in 1985 and are awarded every year to the best books written by British Columbian authors or published by BC firms. The first winners were *Cedar* by Hilary Stewart, *Intertidal Life* by Audrey Thomas, *Duff: A Life in the Law* by David Ricardo Williams and *Islands at the Edge* by the Islands Protection Society.

MUSICIANS

A Good Investment

In 1970, British Columbia couple Terry Jacks and Susan Pesklevits, professionally known as the Poppy Family, spent only $125 to record their song "Which Way You Goin' Billy?" at Vancouver's R & D Studio. The song soon became the number-one hit on the international charts, selling more than three million copies and winning two Juno Awards. Four years later, Jacks (now divorced) surpassed this success with an English-language version of Jacques Brel's song "Seasons in the Sun." That single sold over 13 million copies and earned Jacks another four Junos. Indeed, thanks to "Seasons in the Sun," Jacks sold more records in 1974 than anyone else in the world and became the first Canadian to have two number-one hits on the American charts. Over 30 years later, "Seasons in the Sun" is still the bestselling single ever recorded by a Canadian.

He Calls Vancouver Home
Although born in Kingston, Ontario, musician Brian Adams has called Vancouver home since 1974 and made his first recording there a year later at the tender age of 16. Within eight years, Adams had become an international success, and his 1991 single "(Everything I Do) I Do It For You" still holds the record as the longest-running (16 weeks) number-one song ever on the British pop charts.

The Girl from Nanaimo

One day in the 1980s, legendary jazz bassist Ray Brown stepped inside a Nanaimo restaurant and heard a talented young lady playing the piano. The woman had been born into a family that loved music, and she showed great talent at a tender age. She started classical piano lessons at the age of four, was playing with a local jazz band while in high school and began performing at a Nanaimo restaurant three nights a week when she was only 15. At 17, she won a scholarship to the prestigious Berklee College of Music in Boston and studied there for a year and a half before heading back home to BC. Brown was impressed by what he heard, became the young woman's friend and mentor and introduced her to influential teachers and producers. Later on, the young jazz pianist added singing to her repertoire and released her first CD in 1993. She has released a few more since then, including one that went platinum in the United States and double platinum in Canada. She has also won both the Juno and Grammy Awards for her work, redefined the genre of jazz and made jazz popular again with mainstream audiences—and all before she was 35! Her name: Diana Krall.

The New Sinatra (Thanks to Prime Minister Mulroney)
Burnaby-native crooner Michael Bublé is frequently compared to Frank Sinatra, but success did not come right away. He once won a talent contest, only to be disqualified because he was too young to enter. His grandfather, a plumber who encouraged Bublé's interest in music, worked for free for any musician who'd let his grandson sing a few songs with them on stage. Bublé later won first prize at the Canadian Youth Talent Competition. He went on to perform in a road show, sing in a musical revue and record a couple of albums. He even received two Genie Awards for songs that he wrote for the movie *Here's to Life*. But his big break finally came on September 16, 2000, at the wedding of former Prime Minister Brian Mulroney's daughter, Caroline. Bublé was hired to sing "Mack the Knife," and the ex-PM liked what he heard. The 25-year-old Bublé was soon introduced to

award-winning record producer and music mogul David Foster, and with Foster as producer, a self-titled album, *Michael Bublé*, was released in 2003. It was a tremendous success, going triple platinum in Canada and reaching the bestselling charts in 15 countries (including the number-one spot in Australia). Two years later, the even more successful album, *It's Time*, was released. It went multi-platinum in several countries and was a number-one hit in Canada, Australia, Italy and Japan. The album was also among the top 10 in both the United Kingdom and the United States, and it won Bublé four Juno Awards. All told, Bublé has sold over 10 million recordings worldwide and has fans on every continent. And his single "Home" was the most frequently heard song on Canadian radio in 2005.

A Welcome Nova Scotia Export

Sarah McLachlan started singing when she was only four, and her first instrument was the ukulele. By the time she became a teen, she was taking voice and opera lessons and studying classical piano and guitar at the Nova Scotia Conservatory of Music. McLachlan was discov-ered in 1985 at the age of 17 when she was the vocalist for a Halifax rock group called the October Game. The band was playing its very first concert at Dalhousie University, and in the audience was Mark Jowett of Vancouver's Nettwerk Productions (whose own band was sharing the stage that night). McLachlan was instantly offered a contract, but her parents thought that she was too young and convinced their daughter to stay home and finish her studies at the Nova Scotia School of Art and Design, where she was studying jewellery design. But Nettwerk didn't give up; two years later, McLachlan signed with the record label (before she had written even a single song!) and moved to Vancouver. In 1988, McLachlan's debut album, *Touch*, was released, and it soon reached gold in Canada, eventually hitting platinum. Her 1991 album, *Solace*, was an even bigger success, 1993's *Fumbling Towards Ecstasy* was a multi-platinum international hit and 1997's *Surfacing* went diamond! Since 1988, McLachlan has sold over 22 million records worldwide and has won three Grammy Awards and eight Juno Awards. Someone wrote in McLachlan's high school yearbook that she was destined to be a famous star, and the prediction has come true!

Highland Dance Music Anyone?

Aragon Recording Studios was the first music recording studio in British Columbia. It was established by musician, big band leader and radio deejay Al Reusch in 1946 and originally operated out of a small, three-room office. Best known for recording songs and albums of country and western, folk and early rock musicians (including Diana Ross and the Supremes and Led Zeppelin), Reusch originally created Aragon to record Scottish highland dance tunes. And Reusch wasn't too fond of post-Beatles rock, so he sold the business in 1970, shortly after the Fab Four's breakup. Aragon is now known as Mushroom Studios.

BRITISH COLUMBIA GOES TO HOLLYWOOD

And the Oscar Goes to...

The first British Columbian to be nominated for an Academy Award for acting? That was Vancouver-born John Ireland, who received a Best Supporting Actor Oscar nomination for his role as Jack Burden in the 1949 hit *All the King's Men*. He lost to Dean Jagger, who co-starred in *Twelve O'Clock High*. Ireland starred in almost 200 movies in his long career and was popular in the late 1940s and early 1950s playing heavies and later, tough, cynical, brooding heroes. To date, no one from British Columbia has ever received an Oscar for acting.

Perry Mason was from New Westminster!

Raymond Burr, the Emmy Award–winning actor who played the famous defence attorney on TV from 1957 to 1966 and again in made-for-TV movies in the 1980s and 1990s, was born in New Westminster. Though his parents divorced while he was young, and he was raised by his mother in California, Burr got his start in acting in BC when, at the age of 12, while visiting his father, Burr was hired by a Vancouver theatre company and toured Canada. He was an active promoter of the Canadian entertainment industry and of local BC charities, and his ashes are interred in the city's Fraser Cemetery.

The First Nude in the Movies!

Victoria-born Nell Shipman, silent film star, director, producer and writer, was the first actress in the world to ever do a full frontal nude scene on film. It was in the 1919 movie *Back to God's Country*, which coincidentally (or perhaps because of the scene), became the most financially successful silent film ever made in Canada. The tagline in one of the posters for the movie was: "Is the Nude Rude?"

Actress, Writer, Director, Producer and Animal Lover!

BC's Nell Shipman was not only a silent film star, but also one of the first actresses to write, direct and produce her own movies. As well, she was an animal trainer and donated the animals in her large private zoo to the San Diego Zoo in 1925.

Discovered at Football Game

In 1989, a 22-year-old beauty from Ladysmith was out having fun with her friends at a BC Lions football game. A Jumbotron camera focused on her shapely figure dressed in a Labatt's T-shirt. The fans cheered, and the beer company's advertising executives took notice. The next thing you know, she's doing TV commercials, appearing on the cover of *Playboy* magazine a record six times and becoming an international star on the television series *Baywatch*. Her name: Pamela Anderson.

Alex Keaton was from Burnaby!

Although born in Edmonton, actor Michael J. Fox grew up in Burnaby and started his professional acting career in BC in 1976 with the role of Jamie on the CBC-TV series *Leo and Me*. In fact, Fox seriously considered giving up the role before the series even began! Callbacks were scheduled for the very day that he was to play the lead in his high school's production of

Rumpelstiltskin. Fortunately, the CBC was so impressed with the 15-year-old's first audition that they rescheduled the callbacks just to suit him. The series didn't last long, but Fox continued to perform in local theatre and in various TV shows and movies filmed in BC before dropping out of grade 12 at Burnaby Central High and moving to Hollywood in 1979. Three years later, he got the part of Alex Keaton on the popular TV series *Family Ties*, and the rest (as they say) is history! The community theatre in Burnaby is named after him.

He Was a Real Chief!

Chief Dan George, actor and Academy Award nominee, was a real British Columbia First Nations chief! He was the leader of the Tsleil Waututh (Tsla-a-wat) First Nation, also known as the Burrard band, from 1951 to 1963. In addition, after he became famous as an actor, George was named the honourary chief of both the Squamish and Shuswap bands. Born on Burrard Reserve No. 3 in North Vancouver, sources differ as to whether his original name was Geswanouth Slahoot (which means "thunder coming up over the land from the water") or Tes-wah-no. In any case, he was renamed by missionaries when he was five years old. George lived on the No. 3 Reserve his entire life.

A First Nations Actor Playing a First Nations Character—What an Idea!

British Columbian Chief Dan George's most famous role in the movies was that of Old Lodgeskins in the 1970 film *Little Big Man.* The part earned him an Oscar nomination for Best Supporting Actor, making him the first person from the First Nations to ever receive an Academy Award nomination for acting. (The Oscar that year went to John Mills for *Ryan's Daughter.*) Before George got the role, it was turned down by Sir Laurence Olivier, Paul Scofield and Richard Boone—all non-Natives!

Making the Most of Her Sex Appeal

Best known for playing the femme fatale Samantha on the *Sex in the City* television series, actress Kim Cattrall was raised in Little River on Vancouver Island. She is also the author of two bestsellers: *Sexual Intelligence* (he appears naked on the front cover) and *Satisfaction: The Art of Female Orgasm*. And, at the age of 25, Cattrall dated 61-year-old Prime Minister Pierre Trudeau in 1981 after meeting him at the premiere of one of her first movies, *Tribute*.

A Movie Star Can't Work in Television?
Vancouver-born Yvonne De Carlo is best remember as Lily Munster in the 1960s TV series *The Munsters*, but by then she already had a 20-year career on the silver screen playing opposite such greats as John Wayne, Rock Hudson and Clark Gable in westerns, comedies and adventure films. Because of her ability to speak French, De Carlo was also the first major Hollywood actress to star in a foreign-language film, 1954's *La Castiglione*. She even once dated millionaire, aviator and movie mogul Howard Hughes. And when De Carlo was selected to play Lily Munster, her co-stars Fred Gwynne and Al Lewis were worried about how she would fit in with the rest of the cast; she was, after all, a major movie star while they were merely television actors.

Movie Mogul Mutters BC Girl "The Most Beautiful…in the World!"

BC's Yvonne De Carlo was only a 22-year-old dancer and bit-part actor with over 20 small, uncredited movie roles on her résumé when Hollywood producer Walter Wanger saw her in early 1945 and publicly proclaimed that De Carlo was "the most beautiful girl in the world." He immediately cast her in the lead in his next picture, *Salome, Where She Danced*. The picture was a hit, and De Carlo was an instant success. Vancouver even celebrated "Yvonne De Carlo Week" the following September (her birthday is on September 1) in honour of its native daughter.

Beam Me Up, Scotty!

An expert at foreign accents, Vancouver-born James Doohan made his character on the *Star Trek* TV series (1966–69), Chief Engineer Lieutenant Commander Montgomery Scott, a Scotsman because, in Doohan's words: "All the world's best engineers have been Scottish." And if you closely watch Doohan in the show's most popular episode, "The Trouble with Tribbles," you'll notice that the middle finger of the actor's right hand is missing. He lost that finger as a result of a German machine-gun attack when he was a young soldier at Juno Beach on D-Day in 1944. Doohan died in 2005 and arrangements have been made to fly his cremated remains into space and release them into Earth's orbit.

DID YOU KNOW?

BC actor James Doohan's career spanned over 50 years, but he was typecast thanks to his role as engineer Montgomery Scott on the 1960s sci-fi TV series *Star Trek*. When he made a guest appearance on *Knight Rider 2000*, the credits actually read "Jimmy Doohan, the guy who played Scotty on *Star Trek*." Still, Doohan's performance encouraged many young people to become engineers and that earned him an honourary degree from the Milwaukee School of Engineering.

BC Magician's Fame Spreads to the Comic Pages
Ever read the comic strip *Mandrake the Magician*? It first appeared in 1934 and has been in syndication ever since. The title character, with his top hat, pencil-line moustache and scarlet-trimmed cap, was drawn to look like famous British Columbia magician, Leon Mandrake.

Magoo is from BC!
Remember that popular near-sighted cartoon figure, Mr. Magoo, who was always impervious to the disasters that he was causing all around him? Yep, he's a British Columbian. Or rather, he was the creation of Victoria-born Stephen Bosustow.

HOLLYWOOD COMES TO BRITISH COLUMBIA

Movies Come to BC

Canada's first permanent movie house was Vancouver's Electric
Theatre. Opened in 1902 by John Albert Schulberg, the audience was treated to a short, silent documentary entitled *The
Eruption of Mount Pelee.* The movie was shown every night,
with matinees on Thursdays and Saturdays. Admission was
10 cents. And, to assure the public's sensibilities at the end of
the Victorian Age, the newspaper advertisements for the film
promised viewers that the theatre was "moral and refined."

Beginnings of Hollywood North

The first major Hollywood movie with scenes shot in British Columbia was Frank Lloyd's 1925 silent drama *The Winds of Chance*. The film was based on a popular novel written by Rex Beach. In the movie, Capilano Canyon substituted for the Klondike, and scenes were also filmed in Lytton.

BC's Oscars and Emmies

British Columbia as its own version of the Academy and Emmy Awards. The Leo Awards were established in 1998 to honour the best in BC-made film and television programs. The first movie to win a Leo for best picture was *Rupert's Land*, and the first TV show to win for best series was *Da Vinci's Inquest*.

Swashbuckler Buckled in Vancouver

Although he wasn't born in British Columbia and never lived in the province, years of hard drinking finally caught up with movie swashbuckler Errol Flynn in BC. In 1960, the 50-year-old actor and his 17-year-old "protégé," actress Beverley Aadland, came to Vancouver for a week to sell Flynn's $100,000 yacht to a local businessman. While in town, the star of *Captain Blood* and *The Adventures of Robin Hood* often complained of recurring malaria attacks. Later, as Flynn and Aadland were being driven to the Vancouver airport, the actor complained that he was unable to move his legs, and he was taken to the apartment of a doctor, who proceeded to treat him for a possible slipped disc. While there, Flynn suffered a heart attack (his third in recent years) and died. An autopsy at the Vancouver coroner's office disclosed that Flynn had the body of "a tired old man—old before his time, and sick."

Sci-fi in Burnaby

Ever hear of Amanda Tapping or Michael Shanks? No? Then obviously you're not a fan of science fiction. These British Columbians are stars of the internationally popular *Stargate SG-1* television series filmed at Burnaby's Bridge Studios and other locations across BC's Lower Mainland. Premiering on July 27, 1997, and in 2006, filming its 10th season, *Stargate* is the second longest running sci-fi show in television history; only Britain's *Doctor Who*, which ran for 26 years (1963–89) and was brought back to life in 2005, has a longer history. *Stargate SG-1* is watched in over 10 million households around the world every week. In addition, the show has spawned a successful spinoff television series, *Stargate: Atlantis*, and is the basis for four amusement park rides in Germany and the United States. Over 30 million DVDs of *Stargate* episodes have sold, as well as millions of *Stargate* books, comic books, magazines and other merchandise.

Let's Go to the Café and Visit Nick

Ever want to visit Molly's Reach Café? Or maybe spend the afternoon with your old friend, Nick Adonidas? Well, you can't. The focal point of *The Beachcombers* television series, the café, was actually the old liquor store in Gibsons, and Nick was really BC actor Bruno Gerussi. The show, which was filmed on the Sunshine Coast, ran from 1972 to 1991, was broadcast in 38 countries and was the longest running drama series in Canadian television history. *The Beachcombers* is now in reruns and syndication, bringing British Columbia to millions of viewers around the world.

BASEBALL

What's That Team's Name?

Ever hear of the Vancouver Horse Doctors? How about the Vets? These were the earlier incarnations of the Beavers, Vancouver's first successful professional baseball team. Members of the Northwestern League, they won the league championship three times before disbanding in 1922.

Turn On the Lights!

Like nighttime baseball? You have Vancouver's Bob "Mr. Baseball" Brown to thank for that. The American baseball player came to BC in 1910, when he bought and became manager of the Vancouver Beavers. He would later own the Vancouver Capilanos (another baseball team) and build Athletic Park near False Creek, where professional baseball was played for nearly 40 years. And in 1930, Brown installed giant lights at Athletic Park, making Vancouver the first city in Canada to enjoy nighttime baseball.

HOCKEY

Who Likes the Millionaires?

At a time when the city's population totalled little more than 100,000, the 10,500-seat Denman Arena, where the Vancouver Millionaires played from 1912 to 1922, was regularly filled to capacity.

Go Maroons?

The Vancouver Millionaires won BC's first Stanley Cup championship in 1915, when the team defeated the Ottawa Senators 26–6 in a three-game series sweep. The Millionaires also made it to the finals in 1918, 1921 and 1922. But later in 1922, the Millionaires became the Vancouver Maroons, and Vancouver never won the trophy again in the 20th century, though the Maroons were runners-up in 1923 and 1924.

Victoria's Gift to Hockey

The Victoria Aristocrats, the first and only major professional hockey team in Victoria, became the Victoria Cougars in 1922. Three years later, they won the Stanley Cup, the first and only time the Cup has come to Victoria. But in 1926, all the Pacific Coast Hockey League's players were sold to the NHL, and the Cougars suddenly found themselves playing for Detroit. Eventually, their name was changed to the Red Wings, and under that label, they became the most successful American team in the history of hockey.

Victoria's "Gift" to Junior Hockey

The Cougars resurfaced in Victoria in 1971, but as a junior hockey team. At first, the new team had quite a bit of success, but after the mid-1980s, it was all downhill. The Cougars "scored" the worst record in history, with 5 wins and 65 losses in the 1989–90 season. They also had the greatest losing streak—32 consecutive games—in Canadian junior hockey history. Once the fans deserted the Cougars, the Cougars left Victoria for Prince George in 1994.

CANADA'S OTHER OFFICIAL SPORT: LACROSSE

Who Cares about Hockey? Let's Play Lacrosse!

In the early 20th century, lacrosse was the most popular professional sport played in British Columbia. Its players were paid the highest salaries of any professional athlete in the province, and whenever there was a New Westminster–Vancouver match, an estimated one out of every four of the two cities' 60,000 residents showed up for the games.

Go Salmonbellies!

Canada's most famous professional lacrosse team is probably the New Westminster Salmonbellies. The name was originally meant as an insult (the Vancouver team was likewise known as the Crab Eaters and the Victoria team as the Clam Diggers), but was soon adopted by the team, whose members were proud of their city's role in the fishing industry. The Salmonbellies won their first Minto Cup in 1908, and except for 1911 and 1920, won it every year until 1934. The team also won the gold medal for Canada at the 1908 Olympics in London and tied for first place when lacrosse was a demonstration sport at the 1928 Olympics in Amsterdam. And since 1908, the Salmonbellies have won the Mann Cup a record 24 times!

Over There!

While serving in France in World War I, four Canadian soldiers from Richmond organized a lacrosse league among their comrades in arms. The result: the Canadian Army Corps Lacrosse Championship, which was played "over there" behind the front lines.

Show Me the Money!

Lacrosse was the highest-paying professional sport in British Columbia in the early 1900s. While playing for the Vancouver Millionaires, hockey legend Edouard "Newsy" Lalonde never earned more than $2000 a season, but he was paid up to $5000 (over $45,000 in today's dollars) every summer for playing lacrosse.

A Little Gunplay, Anyone?

Think hockey is violent? Try lacrosse in the early 1900s. During one Vancouver–New Westminster game, the coach of the Vancouver team literally threw three of the New Westminster Salmonbellies over a fence. A week later, Salmonbellies fans pelted that same coach with rotten eggs. The coach then pulled out a pistol and fired into the crowd. No one was hurt, and since violence was an accepted part of the game, no charges were filed either.

You Can't Say That!

Men were not the only ones to play lacrosse. From 1925 until 1939, there was a four-team women's league in the Lower Mainland that often drew crowds of up to 10,000 per game. One of the four teams was the famous Richmond Milkmaids. And the first foul against the Milkmaids was not for crosschecking, tripping or anything like that, but for the use of unladylike language!

OTHER SPORTS AND RECORDS

World's Fastest Man

Despite his slim build (he weighed only 59 kilograms) and a heart damaged by the rheumatic fever that he suffered as a child, Percy Williams of Vancouver became the world's fastest sprinter in 1928, winning gold medals in both the 100-metre and 200-metre sprints at the Olympic Games in Amsterdam. This was the first time that a Canadian had won two gold medals at a single Olympics in track and field, a feat that was not repeated until 1996. He went on in 1930 to win the 100-yard dash at the British Empire (now Commonwealth) Games and set a world record in the 100-metre dash (10.3 seconds) that endured until 1936.

Snooker

Victoria-born Cliff Thorburn (aka "The Grinder") is not a household name, but he is one of the greatest snooker players in history. He won his first North American championship in 1971. Nine years later, he became the first person from outside Britain to win the world championship, and in 1986, the first person in history to win the world master's championship three times. In addition, Thorburn has won the Canadian snooker championship 13 times, the North American championship twice and the Australian Masters once. He also holds the Canadian record of 147 perfect games, including three in only eight days in 1973, and the first in a world championship contest. (Regrettably, to the best of anyone's knowledge, this sports giant is not related to the humble author of this book.)

Commonwealth Games: Precursor to 2010 Olympics?

The first time that British Columbia hosted the Commonwealth Games (which were then called the British Empire and Commonwealth Games) was in 1954, when they were held in Vancouver. That year, Canada won nine gold, 20 silver and 14 bronze medals, coming in third in the total medal count behind England and Australia.

The second time British Columbia hosted the Commonwealth Games was in 1994, when they were held in Victoria. That year, Canada won 40 gold, 42 silver and 46 bronze, coming in second behind Australia in the total medal count.

British Columbia's Bathtub Admiral!

Frank Ney had a distinguished record as a community booster, mayor of Nanaimo and member of the Legislative Assembly. He was also a bathtub admiral! Ney helped organize the 60-kilometre Great Bathtub Race in 1967, in which 212 "tubbers," in all sorts of floating craft, tried to sail across the Georgia Strait from Nanaimo (the "Bathtub Racing Capital of the World") to Vancouver's Fisherman's Cove. Although only 47 "vessels" made it to the finish line, the race was considered a great success. Rusty Harrison, in 3 hours and 26 minutes, was the winner.

The Loyal Nanaimo Bathtub Society was created soon afterwards to continue the race as an annual event, and it named Ney as the Society's first Bathtub Admiral of the Fleet. Giving his role all the seriousness that it deserved, Ney showed up every year in a pirate outfit, complete with a sword, bright red coat and black hat with the skull-and-crossbones on it, to fire the race's starting flare. The races continue even today, but since 1997, the tubbers have sailed a 60-kilometre course that begins in Nanaimo Harbour near Protection Island, goes around Entrance Island, then up and around the Winchelsea Islands and ends on the Departure Bay beach. Every sailor who enters the race receives the Royal Order of the Gold Plug, and each year's winner gets the Silver Order of the Toilet Plunger.

GIVE ME A CALL!

No Long Distance Charges!

British Columbia's first two telephones were built and installed in 1878, but you weren't able to make a long distance call. William Wall, a mechanic at James Dunsmuir's famous coal mine at Wellington, BC, used the information from a recent *Scientific American* magazine article to manufacture the phones. He then connected them to a line between the mine and the loading docks a few kilometres away at Departure Bay.

It's Ringing—One Moment Please

The first trans-Canada phone call was made in 1916 from Vancouver to Montréal. Well, it really wasn't a "trans-Canada" call because phone lines did not yet cross the entire country. The call had to go through Portland, Salt Lake City, Omaha, Chicago and Buffalo before it reached its destination.

DID YOU  KNOW?

BC's first automatic phone exchange—dial telephones for which operators were not needed to place a call—were installed in Victoria in 1930; it took another nine years before they came to Vancouver. Adoption of the new dial phones also meant new telephone numbers for everybody and a new telephone directory.

WONDERS ON WHEELS

What Was that Four-Wheeled Contraption?

The first automobile in British Columbia? It was a Stanley
Steamer purchased and brought to Vancouver by William Henry
Armstrong in 1898. (Some sources say it was in 1899.)

Fill'er Up!

Canada's first gas station opened in Vancouver in 1907, when the
number of gas-powered automobiles in Vancouver skyrocketed
to seven. The station was on the corner of Cambie and Smithe
Streets next to the Imperial Oil Company storage yard. It consisted of a corrugated tin shed that sheltered a barroom chair
and a cushion for its first attendant, Imperial Oil's night watch-
man, who needed a new, daytime job. The gasoline was stored
outside in a 59-litre kitchen hot-water tank fitted with a glass
gauge that was marked with white dots in one-gallon (4.5-litre)
increments. The tank was placed on top of a cement pillar and
connected to a 3-metre-long rubber garden hose, and the attendant would use his fingers and thumb to turn the flow of gas off

and on. Before the station was built, gasoline had to be scooped up with buckets from a large wooden barrel provided at the site by the oil company—a dangerous practice. On a busy morning, the station sold gasoline to three or four cars.

DID YOU KNOW?

On January 1, 1922, a revolution came to automotive driving in British Columbia. That's the day when cars switched from driving on the left side of the road to driving on the right side.

Here Come the Fire Engines!

In 1917, the Vancouver Fire Department retired its last horse and became fully motorized. The process began nine years earlier, when the VFD acquired the first three motorized firefighting units ever made by the Seagrave Company of Columbus, Ohio. It's quite possible that the process was helped by Fire Chief John Howe Carlisle's enthusiasm for motor vehicles; he was the owner of one of the first cars in Vancouver and loved to drive it around town. In any case, Vancouver was the first major city in Canada to have a fully motorized fire department.

The Great Race

Hazelton didn't share in British Columbia's prosperity in 1911, and the local businessmen knew why: there were no roads that were passable by cars to connect the community to the outside world. So the town fathers decided to award $1000 to the first person to drive an automobile to Hazelton under its own power. Soon, the Pacific Highway Association got into the picture and offered a gold medal to the first person to drive from Seattle to Hazelton. (This was all part of the association's push for the construction of a highway from British Columbia to the country of Panama.) The selected route began in Seattle, went east to Ellensburg, Washington, and then north through the Nicola

Valley to Kamloops. At the time, there were no roads yet for cars in the Fraser Valley or in the Okanagan. The contestants would then drive to Ashcroft and along the old Cariboo Wagon Road to Quesnel. From there, the drivers would follow the Yukon Telegraph Line past Fraser Lake, through Aldermere and on to Hazelton. The total distance was 2062 kilometres, including 322 kilometres where no wheeled vehicle, motorized or horse-drawn, had ever been and 644 kilometres that no automobile had ever seen. In addition, the route from Quesnel to Hazelton was, in the best parts, an old wagon trail and, at times, merely a pack trail through dense forest and swamps.

It is not known how many cars started for Hazelton, but the race was soon down to just one vehicle—a Flanders "20" Studebaker driven and owned by the president of one of Seattle's first Studebaker dealerships, P.E. Sands. It would take Sands 37 days to make the trip from Seattle to Hazelton, including the 24 days it would take to travel the 264 kilometres (at an average of only 11 kilometres per day) from Fraser Lake to Aldermere, where there were no roads at all. But in the end, Sands got his money and his gold medal.

Winning Car Sailed Home

In 1911, there were no gas stations in British Columbia north of Ashcroft, so when P.E. Sands of Seattle attempted to become the first to drive an automobile to Hazelton, he added a 136-litre auxiliary gas tank to his Flanders "20" Studebaker and took along a complete set of extra tires. In addition, the fenders of the five-passenger, three-speed vehicle were taken off so the car could drive through the narrow pack trails between Quesnel and Hazelton. The vehicle was also equipped with a block and tackle to get through the mud and axes to widen the "road" when needed. And once he reached Hazelton, Sands did not go back to Seattle the same way that he came. Instead, after he got his money and his medal, Sands and the Studebaker took a stern-wheel steamer down to Prince Rupert and then sailed home.

AIRBORNE...SORT OF

The Twinplane

A dirigible flew over New Westminster in 1909, and the first heavier-than-air aircraft flown over BC (piloted by American pilot Charles Hamilton) took off in front of 3500 spectators on March 25, 1910, from the Minoru Park Racetrack in Richmond. But British Columbia blacksmith and hardware merchant William Wallace Gibson made a much more significant contribution to Canada's aviation history. In 1910, from his Victoria workshop, Gibson designed and constructed the first Canadian-built airplane flown anywhere in the world! He also designed and built the plane's engine, which, by coincidence, was the first successful aircraft engine built in Canada. The engine was an odd-looking, six-cylinder, three-carburetor machine with propellers that rotated in opposite directions at the front and back of the crankshaft.

On September 8, 1910, Gibson took off in his contraption, which he called the "Gibson Twinplane," from the slopes of Mount Tolmie and flew 61 metres. Hey, don't knock it—that's farther than the Wright Brothers went on their first flight! Unfortunately, Gibson forgot to install brakes on his plane. Two weeks after his inaugural flight, he was airborne again, but the Twinplane was destroyed when Gibson couldn't stop the aircraft. He hit an oak tree while landing. That didn't stop Gibson—he just went right ahead designing and building his second flying machine, the Multi-plane.

Air Crash Nearly Caused by a Toque

While millions now travel in comfort every year in a jet or plane, British Columbia's first air passengers in 1912 didn't have it so good. William Stark of Vancouver had just learned how to fly and was the proud owner of a new Curtiss single-seat, pusher-propeller biplane, which he had ordered from the manufacturer in California and then assembled himself at the Minoru Park Racetrack in Richmond. The plane was built of bamboo and wood and held together only by wire and tin fasteners. Its wings were covered with silk, canvas or some other similar material and made airtight with a varnish. A loud Curtiss eight-cylinder, 75-horsepower engine, located almost directly behind the pilot, powered the aircraft. The plane was designed to carry only one person: the pilot! And there was no fuselage or "skin" to the plane to hold everything together and protect the pilot from the wind and weather. Stark planned to become an exhibition and stunt flyer and, as a promotional gimmick, arranged to take Jimmy Hewitt, a newspaper reporter, on a flight with him. To make room for Hewitt, Stark used a rope to attach a piece of board to the upper surface of the wing immediately to the left and behind the pilot's seat. There were no safety straps; Hewitt had to on hold for dear life to the wing strut on his left and the engine beam-brace strut on his right as his legs dangled freely in the air beneath the front of the wing and the wind did its best to push him off.

Right after Hewitt's ride, it was Olivia Stark's turn. No one thought much about it as the Curtiss lifted off, but the large woollen toque that she wore on the flight almost killed her and her husband. The wind blew the headpiece off Mrs. Stark's head and right into the engine's propeller when the couple was about 180 metres in the air. The toque wrapped itself around one of the blades, and the now-unbalanced propeller caused the plane to shake violently until the hat fell off. William Stark didn't know what had happened and was convinced that the entire plane was going to fall apart in the air. Fortunately, the crisis lasted only for a moment, and the Starks made a safe landing. But the toque was never found!

How Long Will the Flight Take?

On August 7, 1919, the first flight over British Columbia and the Canadian Rockies was completed. Captain Ernest Hoy flew a Curtiss JN4 ("Jenny") from Vancouver to Calgary. Flight time: 17 hours!

HOW (AND HOW NOT) TO MAKE MONEY

Whopping Bank Fees

When Canada and the United States signed the Columbia River Treaty in 1964, it was agreed that BC would receive a $273 million payment from the Americans for its downstream rights on the river. In turn, the province was committed to building three dams on the Columbia for electricity generation and flood control. A cheque in U.S. funds for the appropriate amount was deposited into the provincial government's account at the Canadian Imperial Bank of Commerce—and the CIBC charged the province nearly $20 million in fees to convert the payment into Canadian dollars.

DID YOU  KNOW?

For 70 years, from 1879 to 1949, it was illegal to sell margarine in British Columbia. And even now, the law controls the amount of yellow colouring used in its manufacture.

Where to Shop?

The first modern shopping mall in British Columbia? That was the Park Royal Mall in West Vancouver, which opened in 1950. A *Province* columnist at the time described it as the "smartest shopping centre in Canada."

Trains Made Out of Silk!

Well, not exactly. From 1900 until the 1930s, the Canadian Pacific Railway dominated the silk trade between Japan and New York City with its ocean steamers and transcontinental railway connections. Because silk was a highly valuable but perishable commodity, and because insurance was paid on a per diem basis, time was money. Therefore, once the silk arrived at the docks in Vancouver, it was put on special freight trains known as "silk trains" or "silkers" and sent on its way. Each train consisted of seven to 13 cars, and each car contained up to 32 tonnes, or $350,000 worth, of silk. Because of the valuable cargo, armed guards always accompanied the silkers and rarely were there stops at public train stations. The trains were given priority along the entire transcontinental line, allowing the CPR to transport silk from Japan to New York in only 13 days. But Canadian Pacific did not have a monopoly in the business; its competitor, Canadian National, had its own silk trains.

BUSINESS FOLKS

German Financier or Spy?

Alvo von Alvensleben struck it big in Vancouver and lost it all virtually overnight. A German nobleman, he came to the city in 1904 at the age of 25 with only $5 in his pocket. Von Alvensleben's first jobs included barn painting and hunting ducks and geese that he then sold to the Vancouver Club for 35 cents apiece. But thanks to millions in German capital (including $2.5 million from Kaiser Wilhelm II) that he invested in daring land speculation and building projects across BC, within 10 short years, von Alvensleben had created one of the largest financial empires in the province. Unfortunately, he was in Germany when World War I broke out in 1914, and because of the anti-German hysteria of the time, he was not permitted to return home to Canada. The provincial government confiscated von Alvensleben's fortune and property. It was even suspected that he had been a spy! Although von Alvensleben occasionally visited BC after the war, he never lived in Canada again.

Who Needs Two Arms?

Francis "One-Arm" Sutton was already world famous when he came to British Columbia. He built railroads in Argentina and Mexico, lost part of his right arm at Gallipoli, prospected for gold in Siberia, made a fortune betting on horses and in designing and inventing armaments (especially heavy mortars) and became a general in the Chinese army. When he arrived in BC in 1927, he used his wealth to buy Portland Island in the Georgia Strait as well as, for $1 million, the Rogers Building, which was the largest single real estate transaction in Vancouver up to that time. Sutton also actively promoted the idea of opening the Peace River Country to development by extending the PGE Railway (later known as BC Rail) into the area and linking it to Vancouver and Edmonton. His scheme set off a boom in land speculation, and once again, Sutton was the centre of publicity, though he lost every dime he had in the Great Depression. Sutton returned to China in 1931, and during World War II, died in a Japanese prison camp.

It Began with Timber and Booze

The City of Vancouver owes its very existence to a sawmill and a single barrel of whiskey. In 1865, Captain Edward Stamp built a mill on the south shore of Burrard Inlet. At that time, what is now Vancouver consisted of little more than dense forest, and the loggers at Stamp's mill had little alcoholic refreshment available. Two years later, a fat Fraser River boat pilot named Captain John "Gassy Jack" Deighton arrived at the mill in a dugout canoe with his Squamish First Nation wife, his mother-in-law, a dog and a barrel of whiskey. Once on shore, Deighton handed out free booze and promised to run a nearby saloon if the loggers would build it. Deighton House was constructed in less than 24 hours, and Gassy Jack became rich and famous. A small shack-town called "Gastown" soon sprang up around the saloon. In 1870, the town was renamed Granville after a British politician. Fourteen years later, it was incorporated as a city and renamed (for the last time) Vancouver. And the rest is history.

BOOZE AND PROHIBITION

No Beer!

Prohibition came to BC in 1917. The year before, a bill had been approved by the Legislative Assembly banning the sale of alcohol except for medicinal, sacramental and industrial purposes. A public referendum then approved the legislation by a vote of 40,000 to 31,000 in the 1917 provincial election.

However, as in the rest of North America, Prohibition was not a success in British Columbia. The law was difficult to enforce because of its many loopholes. Bootlegging flourished. There was also corruption and scandal. Only three years after its enactment, the voters overwhelming repealed Prohibition—the first province in English Canada to do so—in exchange for a Liquor Control Board and government-run liquor stores. The repeal of Prohibition also marked the beginning of BC's role in running alcohol into the United States, where Prohibition continued for another 12 years. Many of British Columbia's richest families made their initial fortunes during the 1920s in the rum-running business.

No Booze for the First Nations

While it was illegal to sell alcohol to anyone in British Columbia from 1917 to 1921, it was illegal to sell it to anyone of the First Nations from 1854 until 1962.

DID YOU  **KNOW?**

Until 1999, it was illegal for licenced restaurants in British Columbia to sell alcohol without meals or only with appetizers.

The Queen of Rum Row

During the 1920s and early 1930s, over 60 vessels of all sizes from Vancouver, and dozens more from Victoria, the Gulf Islands and the west coast of Vancouver Island, smuggled alcohol into the United States while Prohibition was in effect in America from 1919 to 1933. The most famous of these ships was the *Malahat*. Built in 1917 in Victoria with federal government money, the vessel was a 75-metre-long, five-masted, wooden-hulled auxiliary schooner with two 160-horsepower Bolinder diesel engines. It was designed to transport lumber from BC's sawmills to various communities along the West Coast. But when Prohibition came to America, the *Malahat*, captained by Vancouver's Stuart Stone, became a "mother ship" that sailed the international waters off California, Oregon, Washington and even far-off Hawaii to deliver up to 60,000 cases of Canadian liquor at a time to smaller craft that would then bring the illicit booze to shore. No other "mother ship" brought as much liquor to the "dry" U.S. during Prohibition than the *Malahat*, and the vessel was soon known as the "Queen of Rum Row." When Prohibition ended in 1933, the ship reverted to its original purpose and was turned into the world's first self-propelled, self-loading log carrier. The *Malahat* sank off Barkley Sound in 1944.

EDUCATION

Can I Hear "Pomp and Circumstance" One More Time?

In the late 19th century, most British Columbians (over one-third of whom were single men) cared little for education, and parents were forced to send their children to private schools or outside the province if they wanted their kids to learn more than the three "Rs." But Premier John Robson was a strong advocate for the creation of a public, taxpayer-financed high school system. By the time of his death in 1892, there were high schools in only Nanaimo, Vancouver and Victoria, but nearly 11,000 students attended them—a fourfold increase over the number attending high school in British Columbia just 10 years earlier. In fact, Robson attended every public high school graduation ceremony in the province while he was in office.

Student Protest in the 1920s

Ever hear of the Great Trek? No, it's not another *Star Trek* sequel. In 1922, after years of broken promises from the provincial government, the students at the University of British Columbia were still attending classes in the wards of an unused hospital and in the old army shacks near Vancouver General Hospital. In addition, agriculture classes were held at a private residence, physics and French in the basement of a church and chemistry under a tent, all while nothing was being done to complete the construction of a permanent campus (which had stopped when World War I began) on the 70-hectare site in Point Grey that had been site aside for UBC in 1910. Finally, the students decided to act. They passed around a petition that received 56,000 signatures, which filled seven large suitcases when presented to the Legislative Assembly in Victoria. They also got the support of newspapers, businesses and civic organizations. And then, on October 22, 1922, 1200 students and their supporters held a huge rally in downtown Vancouver and proceeded to march through Kitsilano and Point Grey to the proposed site to pressure the government to act. That did the trick. Funds were appropriated to complete the construction, and in 1925, classes began at the new campus.

AMERICAN "INVASIONS"

Mob Rule

There has been only one known lynching in BC's history. In 1884, 14-year-old Louie Sam from the Sto:lo community of Kilgard, was enticed to cross the border by a job offer from William Osterman, a telegraph operator from nearby Nooksack, Washington. However, once Sam was in Nooksack, Osterman told the lad to "go away," and the young man returned home that night. That same evening, James Bell, a Nooksack shopkeeper, was murdered. Sam was accused of the killing, but the Sto:lo First Nation believed that the Canadian authorities would clear everything up, so they turned the boy over to the police. Sam was in the custody of a Canadian deputy when 100 American vigilantes led by Osterman and his brother-in-law, David Harkness, crossed the border on horseback, threatened the deputy and his family, took Sam and headed back to Nooksack. Just north of the border, the mob stopped and lynched the teenager, hanging him from a tree. To satisfy the Sto:los' demand for justice, two Canadian policemen travelled to Nooksack to investigate the matter. They not only cleared Sam of the crime, but found evidence that the real culprits were Osterman and Harkness. The BC government asked the Washington authorities to turn over the two men for trial for Sam's murder, but that never happened.

A Dying President

The first incumbent U.S. president to visit Canada was Warren G. Harding, who visited Vancouver on July 26, 1923, while on his way to San Francisco from Alaska. (The first future president to "visit" Canada was William Henry Harrison who, as a general, led an invasion of Upper Canada during the War of 1812. But that's another story.) While Harding seemed to enjoy his visit, it was noticed that he appeared pale and tired. A week later, he was dead.

LOVE, BRITISH COLUMBIA–STYLE

The Sanctity of Marriage

The first divorce in British Columbia was granted in 1877. Still, because of the morals of the Victorian Age (and years before the concept of no-fault divorce), the practice did not quickly gain favour. During the next 10 years, only eight other couples were successful in obtaining the dissolution of their marriage in the province.

Personal Ads, 1902

Some people may think that searching for love and affection in personal advertisements is a new thing. They would be very wrong. In 1902, the following ad was published in the *Vancouver Province*:

> *Lady of wealth, attractiveness and good character, somewhat lonely, seeks husband to share her wealth and affections.*
> *Address: Sincere, No. 917, Holland Building, St. Louis, Mo.*

The following advertisement was also printed in the *Vancouver Province* in 1902:

> *A lady stranger in the city and financially embarrassed, wishes to meet a gentleman of means who will assist her.*

A Vancouver employment agency was given as the woman's address. One has to wonder what type of assistance she was looking for.

A ROSE BY ANOTHER OTHER NAME...

Yellow Head

Tête Jaune, the famous guide, hunter, fur trader and trapper of the early 1800s, worked for the Hudson's Bay Company in the area between Jasper and Prince George until his death in 1827. His last cache was located where the town of Tête Jaune Cache now stands, and it's said that he hid a fortune in furs nearby. But Tête Jaune wasn't his real name. The Iroquois Métis guide was actually Pierre Bostonais or Pierre Hastination; records from the period list him as both, and it is unclear which name (if either) was his true identity. In any case, Pierre was nicknamed Tête Jaune, which means "yellow head" in French, by the French voyageurs because of his blond-streaked hair, and the name stuck.

DID YOU KNOW?

Remember David Thompson, the great explorer who crossed the Rockies in 1807 and established a trade route to the Pacific through present-day British Columbia? He may have been born in London, England, but his parents were Welsh, and his real name was Dafydd ap Thomas.

And Your Town Was Named After...

On February 28, 1900, the 120-day siege by the Boers of the British city of Ladysmith in South Africa was finally lifted. Wild celebrations marking the event were held all across the British Empire, including British Columbia. Even the small mining town of Oyster Harbour, south of Nanaimo, got into the act and changed its name to Ladysmith.

If He Wasn't So Hairy

Early fur traders and trappers called the site where Kelowna now stands "L'Anse au Sable" (French for "sandy cove"). It was also called "Okanagan Mission" after a Roman Catholic mission that was built there in 1859. But in the 1860s, the location acquired a third, radically different name. August Gillard moved into the area in 1862 and lived in a structure similar to a First Nations *kekuli* or *kickwillie*, a building that was half shack, half underground dugout, near the present-day bridge at the south end of Kelowna's Ellis Street. Gillard also had a great deal of body hair. One day, as he was crawling out of his home, some passing First Nations people noticed Gillard's resemblance to a bear coming out of its den. They laughingly cried out *Kemxtus! Kemxtus!* (which means "black bear's face"). The word was quickly anglicized to "Kimach Touche," and both Gillard and his residence became known by that moniker. Thirty years later, as the new townsite of Kelowna was being laid out, the city fathers wondered what to call their community. Gillard's story was recounted and Kimach Touche was considered, but was deemed too common, crude and undignified. Instead, the name "Kelowna" was chosen, which in the local Okanagan First Nation language means "female grizzly bear," and was initially pronounced so the second syllable rhymed with "allow."

ATTENTION STAMP AND COIN COLLECTORS!

BC's Answer to Nova Scotia's *Bluenose*

The BCP *No. 45*, of course! The 14-metre-long wooden fishing boat was built in Coal Harbour in Vancouver in 1927 and sailed along the province's coastal waters until it was donated to the Vancouver Maritime Museum in 1990. A 1958 photograph of the ship, taken near Ripple Rock by George Hunter, appeared on the back of the Canadian five-dollar bill from 1972 until 1986.

When $20 is Worth Over $150,000!
If you ever find a British Columbia coin from 1862, don't spend it! That year, the mainland colony issued a handful of $10 and $20 gold and silver coins. In 1999, one of the $20 pieces sold for US$149,500.

Hold On to Your Money

In addition to some gold and silver coins, the BC colonial government also issued $34,000 worth of paper money in 1862 in $5, $10 and $25 denominations. However, except for one copy of each bill that has been saved as a specimen by the provincial government, none of these notes is known to have survived.

Your Money's No Good Here
In the early 1860s, both in British Columbia and on Vancouver Island, it was common practice for banks to issue their own paper money. However, these currencies were unsecured; that is, the banks did not have any insurance to back up the value of the notes in times of trouble. One of the largest banks was owned by Alexander Macdonald and was known as Macdonald & Co. On September 23, 1864, its Victoria branch was robbed of $30,000, and despite great efforts to save it from the blow, the bank eventually went bankrupt. And when it did, everybody with Macdonald's bank notes in their wallet found that they now had nothing but worthless scrap paper.

Save Those Stamps!

Before BC joined Confederation in 1871, the colonies of Vancouver Island and British Columbia both issued postage stamps. Most of these show the image of a crown on top of the letter "V," while others have a portrait of Queen Victoria. But don't use them to mail your letters! Depending on which stamp you have and its condition, it could be worth up to $50,000!

ABOUT THE AUTHOR

Mark Thorburn

Mark Thorburn loves history. He has contributed to and edited several history textbooks and references and has written for newspapers across North America. Mark has lived life as a lawyer, a circuit judge, a college instructor and a historian as well as an author. His educational background is broad, with a BA in political science, a Doctor of Jurisprudence and two MA degrees in American and Canadian history. In his free time, Mark plays sports, reads great books, goes to the theatre and watches classic films. He also like hanging out at some of Vancouver's well-known spots, including Gastown, Stanley Park, Granville Island and Robson Street.

ABOUT THE ILLUSTRATORS

Pat Bidwell

Born and raised in Edmonton, Pat has always had a passion for drawing and art. Initially self-taught, pat completed art studies in visual communication in Edmonton in 1986. Over the years, he has worked both locally and internationally as an illustrator/product designer and graphic designer, collecting many awards for excellence along the way. When not at the drawing board, Pat pursues other interests solo and/or with his wife, Lisa.

Roger Garcia

Roger Garcia immigrated to Canada from El Salvador at the age of seven. Because of the language barrier, he had to find a way to communicate with other kids. That's when he discovered the art of tracing. It wasn't long before he mastered this highly skilled technique, and by age 14, he was drawing weekly cartoons for the *Edmonton Examiner*. He also taught himself to paint and sculpt. Currently, Roger's work can be seen in a local weekly newspaper and in places around Edmonton.